A DICTIONARY OF
NEW THOUGHT TERMS

*THE WORDS AND PHRASES
COMMONLY USED IN METAPHYSICS*

ERNEST HOLMES

DeVorss *Publications*

ISBN: 0-87516-632-6

Second Printing, 1998

*Special thanks to Dr. Robert H. Bitzer, whose generosity inspired
this publication project and whose advice helped guide it,
and to Dr. Craig Carter for sage counsel.*

DeVorss & Company, Publisher
P.O. Box 550
Marina del Rey, CA 90294

Printed in The United States of America

A Word from the Publisher

Ernest Holmes first brought out his *New Thought Terms and Their Meanings* in 1942, citing the fact that "new philosophies, new sciences, and new outlooks upon life make necessary a new terminology"; and he added: "New ideas are frequently misrepresented by the very terms used to express them."

Having himself pioneered many of these same terms, he must have known this from much first-hand experience. It is a tribute to him, as well as to several other great figures who taught New Thought in those earlier days of the Movement, that so many of the terms included here are well known and still current.

Yet even for the person conversant with them, this work holds added value and interest, for it is very much more than a mere dictionary. It can be read consecutively almost as a collection of mini-essays—short, to-the-point gems on the basics and beyond of New Thought, metaphysics, and the Science of Mind. Thus the reader seeking further insight into *treatment* will find no fewer than 20 entries, each taking up the subject from a different angle. And the topical range of the entries is similarly impressive.

As a consequence of Ernest Holmes' ability to conceive a dictionary that reads so much more interestingly and enjoyably than one experiences with most reference works, his key entries are sometimes rather subjectively given, as when *mental* is the first word of an entry that one might seek under some other words coming after it. Thus when we consult *mental treatment,* we get 10 entries in addition to those given under *treatment* alone. Therefore, to strengthen the dictionary and to make it more useful, several hundred cross-references have been introduced.

When a number of cross-references appear after an entry,

they are separated by semicolons (;) never by commas. The individual cross-reference itself frequently appears in shortened form, e.g. *faith overcomes* for *faith overcomes fear.*

This long-out-of-print reference and study work is presented otherwise unchanged except for a very few modest emendations as well as the omission of: (1) terms like *addict, anthropology, clinic,* which are not peculiar to New Thought and which can be found in a general dictionary, and (2) terms strictly psychological in character, of which many were in vogue at the time this book was first published, having since fallen into obscurity or outright disuse.

By way of contrast, almost all of the hundreds of New Thought, metaphysical, and Science of Mind terms and expressions continue in use, and all of these have been retained in this new edition. They will be found to clarify, and elaborate on, not only the teachings and works of Ernest Holmes—most especially his classic *The Science of Mind*—but also those of countless other teachers and authors who have labored in this same broad field during the past century and a half.

ARTHUR VERGARA
Editor

A Dictionary of
New Thought Terms

A

Abiding Presence The Spirit of God, which permeates everything.

Absolute, the The God principle, the Supreme, the Unknowable, Unthinkable, Unmanifest—yet manifest in all. The Unconditioned, yet in every condition. That which is back of all that is manifested, in all universes, known and unknown to man. That which is all Life, all Power. The Formless, which is all form. The Changeless, which includes all change. The Infinite Life Principle, omnipresent, omnipotent, omniscient. The Great Self-Existent Cause back of all that is.

In speaking of "treating in the Absolute," we mean dealing with the Law back of material form; working in the higher planes of thought for the control of conditions on the manifest side of life. "Working in the Absolute" means attuning oneself to the invisible; contemplating the qualities which we believe to be a part of God, such as Love, Harmony, Peace, Wisdom, Strength, etc., and then seeing oneself as partaking, and being a part, of that Infinite Perfection. (See *treating in the.*)

Absolute and relative Refers to the Unconditioned Cause and any effect which It may project. (See *relative.*)

Absolute, treating in the See *treating in the.*

Absolute (the)—understanding of the Absolute is our relative See *understanding of.*

Absolute (the), we cannot contract See *we cannot contract.*

abstract In the realm of the formless; apart from any particular object, as in the realm of ideation. The general, in contradistinction to the particular; as beauty, love, honesty, courage, etc. Abstract thought is in the higher ranges of thought, rather than in the concrete, as in particular objects.

abundance See *"Whosoever hath."*

abundance, identical with thought of Since thought produces fact, then fact must be like the thought which produces it. Hence a thought of impoverishment would create an impoverished condition, while the recognition of abundance would inevitably produce abundance.

acceptance See *bowl of acceptance; intellectual acceptance; mind cannot; subjective acceptance; unbelief; meditation without.*

accidents, purposive See *purposive.*

accumulated consciousness The sum total of one's mental life.

accumulated consciousness of the race thought Sum total of all beliefs which the race has ever held, more or less operating through all of us, unconsciously.

"Acknowledge Him and He shall direct thy paths" Truth, known, automatically becomes demonstrated.

acknowledgment of good makes possible its manifestation Acknowledgment is recognition; and recognition, realized, becomes embodiment.

"Act as though I am and I will be" A mystical presentation of the Law of mental correspondents.

action, rest in The Laws of Mind work smoothly, harmoniously, and without effort. Spiritual Mind treatment should be spontaneous and not laborious.

action, the only ultimate See *thought processes*.

active ideas of truth A spiritual treatment is a definite statement, an active state of consciousness created for a definite purpose.

active right thinking Mental treatment is an active thing; it sets about to demonstrate or prove a certain point in Mind through the definite activity of consciousness. Treatment is always active; it is never day-dreaming.

Adam Undeveloped, or unenlightened man. The opposite of the Christ Principle, as "in Adam all sin, so in Christ all are made free from sin" (1 Cor. 15:22).

Adam as Christ The first Adam is of the earth; the second Adam is the Lord from heaven. *Adam as Christ* means lifting up the principle of Reality within us to a comprehension of its union with Spirit.

Adam consciousness Symbol of the intellect functioning from a material basis. The Life Principle viewed from its lowest angle. Separation, disunity, dissolution.

Adam is transformed into Christ That which seems human and disunited from the Divine automatically becomes transmuted into the Christ through spiritual recognition. It is written that the first Adam is of this earth, the second Adam is the Lord from heaven.

Adam-Kadmon In the Kabalah this term means the ONE (son) of the Divine Father. (AD, in Assyrian, means

Father; in Aramaean AD means "One." AM or OM means the divine, or Deity.) Adam Kadmon has been referred to as the "Heavenly Man," symbolizing the entire humanity and beyond, the Universe itself in a single aspect. The vehicle of the Logos is manifestation.

adversary, the apparent Any belief in the reality of evil.

affirmation in mental treatment Affirming the Divine as the only Presence. That is, affirming the presence of whatever ought to be.

affirmation of truth Any statement which affirms the supremacy of good or which denies the reality of that which is contrary to good. (See *spiritual affirmations; transforming.*)

affirmation, supreme See *supreme affirmation.*

affirmations, subconscious denial of See *subconscious denial.*

affirmative factor The invisible Power that concentrates primordial substance into new forms. It is the principle of the unfoldment of life through the Intelligence that permeates all space, the very Nature of Being Itself as Subjective Intelligence. Cooperating with It, man may create his world of perfection.

Affirmative, the Great: I AM The Principle of Being that expresses Itself as form, on all planes and in varying vibratory force, up through all strata of life, from the rock to liberated man, and beyond. Man's use of the words "I AM" becomes in him the Great Affirmative.

age The measure of long periods of time, such as the Azoic Age (the beginning of life on the planet), the Pliocene Age, Stone Age, Iron Age, Golden Age, Age of Science, the Dark Ages, etc. In Hindu literature an age is called the Day and Night of Brahma. The Outbreathing of a universe is called a Manvantara, the Inbreathing a

Pralaya, or Dissolution. In Truth there is no beginning or end, for there was never a commencement of life, in the Eternal, and there will never be an ending. An Age is man's measure of a period of experience.

agnosticism (agnostic) The doctrine that neither the nature nor the existence of God nor the ultimate character of the universe is knowable. Any doctrine which affirms that all knowledge is relative and uncertain.

"Agree with thine adversary quickly" We arrive at correct spiritual conclusions through agreeing with the Divine Presence in everything.

akasha Space, or ether, as a mind principle.

alchemy A medieval science, the object of which was to try to transmute base metals into gold. In the life of the metaphysician, the term *alchemy* is used in referring to the transmutation of the lower nature (that is, the qualities of ruthless selfishness, greed, cruelty, etc.) into the perfect spiritual Form, toward which man is evolving. The uncovering of the God-self, which already exists, potentially, in each one. This alchemy, or transmutation, is an actual chemical change in the cells of the body, through the use of mental law and high spiritual aspiration. Love is referred to as the Great Alchemist, since where Love is manifest, harmony and right action follow. The vibratory forces of the body are lifted and changed into higher and finer rates of vibration. This is the basis for the panacea of the Elixir of Life, which is eternal youth, so long sought for.

all is mental or spiritual Not only is the invisible Principle of Life a thing of mind and spirit, form also is mental and spiritual. It is Spirit caught in a temporary mold for a definite purpose.

all is Mind All creation is Mind in form and responsive to the Intelligence which creates it. This same Intelligence in us therefore responds to us. Immanuel Kant said that we are able to recognize an apparently external object by reason of the fact that it awakens an intuition within us.

"All rivers run into the sea . . . thither they return again" Refers to the unity of all life; we proceed from Spirit and return to It and are always in It.

"all things . . . ye shall ask . . . believing, ye shall receive" Refers to the immutable Law of Cause and Effect, which returns to us exactly what we set in motion in it.

all thought is creative It would be impossible to assume that one type of thought would be creative without assuming that all types must be.

Alpha and Omega This symbolizes all that God is—Spirit, Matter. The first and the last, and all that lies between. The beginning and the end.

altar Symbolizes spiritual idealism upon which are sacrificed the lower forms of thought.

analogous Similar or bearing some similarity. The principle that like attracts like, in that we attract that to which our thought is attuned.

analogy That which resembles something else. An agreement between two things in some ways, but not identically. In metaphysical teaching, stories are told which bear a resemblance to the thing being illustrated, in order to clarify the thought on the subject at hand. The teachings of Jesus are filled with analogies.

analytical realization Realization arrived at by analysis, argument, process of thought, etc. (See *mental analysis.*)

Ancient of Days God, Spirit, Reality; that which never changes.

ancient wisdom The continuous stream of Truth that has

run through all the great spiritual and philosophic teachings from times of antiquity. The Wisdom of the Ages.

androgynous Having the characteristics of both sexes. The Father-Mother God Principle.

anemia, spiritual treatment for Recognition of the flow of Life, Love, Happiness, and Fulfillment.

angel Symbolizes spiritual influences; angel of the higher self; the Presence of God in man as Christ.

angels ascending and descending Intuition informing the intellect.

animal consciousness The feeling consciousness. Our communication with animals is through feeling. An animal will attack a person who fears it, because the feeling of fear is transferred to its consciousness, and it attacks in self-defense. It is the animal consciousness in man, the consciousness of the physical body itself, that is responsible for deep-seated fears, especially the fear of death. This consciousness is controlled through the mental faculties, through the reasoning mind—the next step up in vibration.

Anointed, the Refers to the consciousness of the Indwelling Christ.

anointing with oil Becoming conscious of the Divine Presence.

anti-Christ Any attempt to use spiritual power for a destructive purpose.

apparent separation Any thought or appearance which causes us to believe that we are separated from the Divine Presence.

appearance Any objective manifestation which may or may not be considered true to the spiritual Reality. (See *"Judge not according."*)

approaching the Spirit See *faith—approaching.*

archetypal man Spiritual man viewed generically, in whose image all men are formed. The universal man. The image and likeness of God.

archetype The ideal form, written about by Plato. The eternal, perfect concept of things, existing in the Mind of God, or Universal Mind, after which form is patterned. The perfect pattern of a thing in thought.

argument, correct Refers to the mental process of thought in spiritual treatment whereby one argues toward the realization of the supremacy of good, the unity of man with God, etc.

argument, false Arguing mentally from the standpoint that there is a dual universe, that there is something opposed to good, etc. (See *false argument.*)

argument logically presented to Mind In treating through argument, one seeks to establish a certain position in his own thought. Hence, he goes through a logical argument within himself in order to establish such a position. The conclusion of his argument constitutes its power and guarantees its results.

argument of doubt Any mode of thought which denies us the privilege of accomplishing a healing or of making demonstrations for ourselves or others. This arises out of the race consciousness.

argument of error Subjective thought patterns of experience resisting any attempt to neutralize them.

arguments—arranging them to meet the need Arranging thought in such a way as to repudiate certain beliefs or fundamental erroneous conclusions about the condition you wish to change.

arguments—conform them to meet needs In mental treatment when one is using the argumentative method, his specific arguments meet—that is, cover—the case by recognizing what ought to be denied and what ought to be affirmed.

arguments—conform them to the theory of perfection The entire body of a mental treatment must be built upon the supposition of Perfect God, Perfect Man, and Perfect Being.

ark Symbol of the Spiritual Principle which rises upon the sea of psychic confusion.

Ark of the Covenant The Principle of Unity within us; the Holy of Holies; the Secret Place of the Most High; the Sacred Name; the Scroll of Life; the realization that God and man are One.

arteries as a spiritual idea Represent a perfect, unobstructed, flexible medium for the flow of Spirit.

"As a man thinketh in his heart" Continual thinking, willing, knowing, or believing creates subjective thought patterns which, in their turn, attract or repel.

"As he thinketh in his heart so is he" As the inner state of consciousness is, so will the condition become.

"As thou hast believed so be it done unto thee" This refers to cause and effect. Any belief in consciousness produces a condition exactly corresponding to such belief.

ascending and descending scale of consciousness The One Mind manifest in everything from the atom to the highest form of intelligence.

ascending arc of the circle A term used to symbolize the evolutionary Force, both personal and cosmic, by which the individual rises from gross materiality into the realm of pure Spirit. The resurrection principle. (See *descending arc of the circle.*)

ascension from the valley of negation to the mountaintop of realization Represents the unfolding of consciousness as it leaves behind its limited patterns of thought and endeavors to sense its unity with the boundless whole.

ascetic One who devotes himself to a solitary and contemplative life; one who practices extreme rigor and self-denial.

asceticism Refers to the doctrine that the material or carnal world is evil or despicable, and that salvation is gained by mortification of the flesh.

"Ask in faith nothing wavering" True prayer is not a petition but a complete and unqualified acceptance.

asking according to His Will This means according to the nature of Reality.

assimilation and elimination Metaphysically interpreted, this means the circulation of Truth eliminating anything unlike Itself.

atomic intelligence The primary Intelligence inherent in the very substance of things; the Intelligence in the atom that keeps it revolving around its central unit of power. This Intelligence is characterized by responsiveness, which may be made use of in healing work. Every atom in every cell of the body has intelligence.

atonement The old Jewish doctrine of redemption through suffering or sacrifice to expiate for a sin. To make amends for an offense. We all atone for wrongdoing, in that the Law of Cause and Effect punishes us until we learn to stop making mistakes. Metaphysical students now realize that the only atonement—that is, the real redemption—is an At-One-Ment with Life Itself, God. Through unity the old accounts are settled and dissolved.

attachment To be bound by sense objects, so that it is painful to be without them.

attitude, mental This is determined by the trend of thought of the individual. One may have an optimistic or completely negative attitude in his approach to life, which makes for his success or failure. All man's experiences come out of his mental attitude.

automatic writings Written messages received when one is controlled by some psychic influence, which many believe may emanate from oneself, those around one, or discarnate spirits.

autosuggestion One's thoughts acting upon one's own mind.

Averages, Law of That Law through which the Great Cosmic Intelligence works in perpetuating races and types through evolution. Through this Law vast numbers of plants, animals, men, etc., are created, which allows for a margin for the destruction of great numbers through accident, etc., but ensures the survival of the type or race because of the vast numbers created. This Law keeps a normal proportion of the race. Through this Law the Universal Intelligence works for the advancement of the race, irrespective of wishes or individuals. If one's wishes are in line with the forward and upward evolutionary movement of the Divine Principle, all the power of the Principle carries him forward. If his desire is opposed to It, he collides with the Great Law and is hurt or destroyed by It. (See *Law of Averages*.)

"Awake thou that sleepest . . . and Christ shall give thee light" This passage implies that the human consciousness is in a dream state from which Christ or Divine Sonship must awaken it. Christ is light. We have the mind of Christ. The mind which Jesus used is Christ; this Mind is in all of us.

B

baptism by fire The purging of the conscious and unconscious processes of thought whereby mental patterns are transmuted from a material into a spiritual consciousness.

baptism by the Holy Ghost Pure spiritual intuition transcendent of intellectual processes. The Light of Heaven. A state of consciousness which is no longer a symbol nor a purging, but which is a deep interior awareness of peace, poise, power, wholeness, and perfection.

baptism by water Symbolic of one's consciousness that he is immersed in Life—liquid Spirit.

"Be ye doers of the Word" We must consciously use Law and demonstrate the Principle.

"Be ye perfect . . . even as your Father which is in heaven is perfect" Means be perfect physically even as you already are spiritually perfect.

becoming as a little child Having implicit and childlike confidence in eternal Goodness and in the ever creative Law.

becoming God-conscious Becoming aware of the Invisible Presence which permeates everything with the essence of perfection, truth, beauty, and power.

"Before they call I will answer" Cause and Effect are one and the same thing: While we are yet speaking the Law is set in motion.

Beginning, in the The starting point of any creation. That out of which all experience is projected.

Being In its absolute sense, God, Spirit, Reality. (See also *Truth of being.*)

belief and believer are one The condition is thought or belief in form; the two are one.

belief and not the thing believed in is the power Since the world has had many varying religious convictions, and since all faiths have produced results, it follows that it is belief itself and not some peculiar religious conviction which gives power to thought.

belief as law When Jesus announced, ''It is done unto you as you believe,'' he was announcing the Law of Belief.

belief, change of Changing our psychological patterns of thought to the acceptance of that which includes the All-ness of God, relative to any fact or experience.

belief displaced by spiritual idea Nothing real is destroyed in spiritual mind practice; it is the material sense of things that is transformed into spiritual realization.

belief, false See *false belief.*

belief, handling See *handling a belief.*

belief in evil creates evil Wherever we place our mental attention, there we tend to create conditions which correspond to such mental attention.

belief is a certain way of thinking No matter how spiritual the belief or the faith may be, it is still an act of consciousness, hence it can be reduced to a state of thought.

Belief, Law of Belief creates its own law, which is changed only by reversing the belief.

belief, separating the See *separating.*

belief, understanding and See *understanding and.*

beliefs, discordant See *separate.*

believe in your heart Refers to the positive inner conviction.

"Believe not every spirit" This refers to the psychic confusion of believing that subjective forms are always what they claim to be.

believing the Truth and believing in Truth To believe in Truth is to recognize or accept spiritual power as Reality. To believe the Truth is to use this power which we believe in.

Beloved Son The divine unique individualization of God which every man is. (See *Only-Begotten Son; Father and.*)

"beside Him there is none other" God manifest and God unmanifest constitutes the totality of Being. God is around and through everything both immanent and transcendent.

Bible The sacred book or books of any race of people; a book containing the sacred writings of any religion, which is used as an authority.

black magic An inverted use of the creative Power of Mind. A determination to use self-will to force others to comply with one's own wishes. Instead of using the Power to cooperate with the forward, evolutionary movement of Life Itself, in unity with Wholeness, which is the Will of God, the Nature of which is toward good for all, the person has the erroneous idea that he can control mind and bend others to his individual will. He manipulates others through what he thinks in his mind. There is but One Mind, which we all use, and only if It is used according to Its Law of Good, of Unity and Wholeness, may we avoid destruction. The wrong use of mind destroys the ignorant one, and he retrogrades instead of moving forward.

blessing Constructive thought directed toward any person or any condition; any constructive thought designed to be helpful.

blind force and Infinite Intelligence Blind force refers to the Law of Cause and Effect, which is a doer and not a knower. Infinite Intelligence refers to limitless capacity consciously to know.

blood Symbol of Divine Life manifesting Itself on the physical plane.

Boaz One of the two great Pillars of the Universe that stood at the entrance to the Temple of Solomon, described in the Bible (1 Kings 7:21; 2 Chron. 3:17). Boaz symbolizes the personal element, also the Voice, or the Word. In Masonic teaching these two pillars represent the Law and the Word before the Temple of Truth. They are united by the Royal Arch of Love, and it is taught that progress in Truth is made by finding the balance between them— that is, to balance the personal with the impersonal, the Great Universal Power. (See *Jachin*.)

body, etheric See *etheric body*.

body, false belief about See *false belief about*.

body is mental and spiritual Body is not to be denied; we are to affirm that body is a combination of spiritual ideas harmoniously expressing life.

Body of Christ The Body of Christ is the immortal individuality within us, manifesting Itself on any particular plane upon which we may be living. The Spiritual Body.

Body of God The entire manifest creation.

body of right ideas In treatment the body is viewed as a combination of spiritual ideas harmoniously unified with the Divine Life.

body, physical See *physical body never denied*.

body, psychic See *psychic body*.

body, spiritual See *spiritual body*.

Body, there is but one Refers to the Body of spiritual ideas. Spiritual Body is a divine idea forever embodying Itself in temporary form. (See *One Body; only One Body*.)

bondage not God-ordained The principle of freedom cannot create bondage or limitation. Bondage is the result of a wrong perception of the principle of freedom.

born again, to be A resurrection from the belief that we are separated from God or Perfect Life into the understanding that "Beloved, *now* are we the sons of God!"

bound by mortal belief To be controlled by race suggestion.

bound by our own freedom Mind is "the law that binds the ignorant and frees the wise." The thought of limitation creates limitation; the thought of freedom creates freedom. Since limitation is a limited viewpoint of Reality, a greater viewpoint automatically heals the limitation. Thus, we are apparently bound and actually set free by one and the same Law.

bowl of acceptance Refers to our mental attitudes, which, as it were, are held up that the outpouring horn of plenty may fill them.

Bread of Heaven The Truth as spiritual food for the soul. (See *"I am the bread."*)

breath The Life of all beings; symbolic of spiritual action which breathes thought into form and withdraws form into thought. The word *Spirit* comes from the Latin word *spiro*, meaning breath. We read in the Bible that "God breathed into man the Breath of Life, and man became a living being." To breathe is to live. Every living thing is a part of the Great Breath, from the very plants, up through the animal kingdom, to man. The breath is a part of the Action of God in man and is quite beyond man's control. In ancient teachings we are told the Great Breath was the beginning of life and energy on the planet. "And the Spirit of God [the Breath] moved upon the waters."

burning bush Refers to the thought that all nature is alive with the Divine Presence. It is the recognition of this Divine Presence which causes the voice to proceed from nature. That is, we commune with God through nature.

business, healing See *healing a sick business.*

business is a thing of thought It would be impossible for one with a negative thought to have an active business. By the same token a negative business is revived through the activity of thought.

"by man came death . . . also the resurrection" Refers to the idea that death is not in the Principle of Truth, but merely in experience; resurrection is an experience of waking from the belief in death.

"By their fruits ye shall know them" Invisible causes are known by studying their effects.

"By thy words thou shalt be justified, and . . . condemned" Refers to the Law of Cause and Effect as It operates upon our thought.

C

case history Refers to the previous experience of the individual one is treating.

"Cast thy burden upon the Lord" Means to depend upon the Law.

"Cast your net on the right side" In this parable Jesus shows that abundance of supply appears when we entertain a consciousness of abundance.

casting out devils Dispelling illusions. Healing the thought of a belief in any form of obsession.

caught in the picture Accepting negative environmental conditions as being laws of restriction, limitation, etc. Refers to the idea of one's becoming so enmeshed in objective circumstances and in thought patterns that he has a complete fixation and is bound by the very Principle which could free him.

Causation, Absolute: not in relation to anything other than Itself Since everything flows from the Absolute, and since the Absolute Itself is the cause of everything that is relative, it follows that the Absolute is not conditioned, limited, or circumscribed by anything that is relative, hence nothing hinders the manifestation of Its thought.

causation, the higher realm of Assumes that all true causation is spiritual and perfect; contradicts anything in mind which denies this and affirms the supremacy of any thought which acclaims the Allness of Good. (See *Spirit is the realm.*)

Cause and Effect All causes are invisible. All effects are results of the invisible taking temporary form. From the standpoint of a mental treatment, Cause and Effect means the idea involved in treatment operating through the Creative Principle to produce a logical manifestation.

Cause and Effect, impersonal Law of The laws of nature have neither feeling, sentiment, nor emotion. The Laws of Mind, like other laws in nature, are always impersonal.

Cause and Effect in the mental world Intelligence, operating through the act of interior awareness, sets a sequence in motion which is called Cause and Effect. Cause and Effect, therefore, are but two ends of a sequence set in motion by the act of self-awareness. Hence, Intelligence, which is the starting point, acting through self-awareness creates any particular sequence of Cause and Effect, but of itself is subject to no law of Cause and Effect. This will explain that the Karmic law binds the ignorant and frees the wise.

Cause and Effect, Law of See *Law of Cause and Effect; Cause and Effect, impersonal Law of.*

Cause and Effect, sequence of We start with pure Intelligence which conceives an idea. This idea which is Mind in action, acting as Law, produces form. Hence the sequence is: Intelligence, idea, law, and form. (See *mental law is; sequence of causation.*)

Cause and Effect, Spirit is both See *Spirit is both.*

Cause and Effect, Truth is both See *Truth is both.*

Cause and Effect—two ends of the same thing Since effect flows out of cause, it is already involved within it. That is, any given cause is certain to produce its logical result unless intercepted.

Cause, First See *First Cause.*

cause, in treatment not necessary to know the specific See *treatment—in.*

Cause, Medium, and effect Spirit—Law—manifestation.

cause must have an effect If there were no effect there could be no cause. Since there is Causation, there must be effect, else Causation would not fulfill Its own nature. Cause and effect must be one.

Cause, Relative First That principle in man by means of which he uses the creative Power to initiate a new series of events in order to bring about a desired condition. It is First Cause, in that it is the creative Power, and relative because it is man's individual use of it.

cause, secondary This is the region of reflections, illusion, the changing, the form side of life. When a new idea is initiated, it creates conditions, which, in turn, produce further conditions. These conditions, which become causes of other conditions, are referred to as Secondary Causation.

Cause, unconditioned The Principle of Mind as Absolute Causation is unconditioned by any existing circumstances; It knows only Its own ability to do, and it is impossible for It to realize any destruction, limitation, or opposition.

Causeless Cause That which, having no cause before It, Itself is the Cause of everything created. Same as First Cause.

causes and conditions Conditions flow out of causes and are created by them. There can be no condition without a cause. Nothing in the visible world is self-caused. From the standpoint of mental treatment, the treatment is the cause, the demonstration is the effect. It is a mathematical necessity.

Celestial World That which is looked upon as a perfect state of being. Heavenly.

Center and the Source The Spirit is centered within us and is the Source of all good.

center, finding one's See *finding.*

center of God-Consciousness Refers to the individualized mind as a manifestation of God. (See *man as a center.*)

"certain (a) man had two sons" Refers to the possibility of dual experience inherent in all people.

chance See *Law of Chance; mental treatment not.*

Changeless Reality Refers to the essence of Being, in which all change takes place; that which of Itself cannot change.

changing our position in the Law No matter what use we have been making of the Law of Cause and Effect, either consciously or unconsciously, in ignorance or through wisdom, we can always start a new sequence and thereby reverse the old causation. (See *deliberately changing our position.*)

changing the belief To reverse fear with faith, the idea of hell with the idea of heaven, etc.

channel for the Divine Faith, expectation, and acceptance automatically demonstrate good.

channel or instrument of God The mind of man measures out the Divine Gifts at the level of man's understanding and of his embodiment of the Divine Nature.

chemicalization Subjective thought disturbance which sometimes takes place as old thought patterns rise to the surface to be replaced by new ones.

child-like mind A mental attitude of unquestioned faith; simple, direct, and joyously expectant.

choice See *personal choice.*

Christ Divine Sonship. The Spiritual Principle in man. The presence of God in man as man. The true man, the Real man, the eternal man. The consciousness of God with us and in us. (See *"I can do."*)

Christ, Blood of Symbolic of the Divine Life individualized and flowing through all people.

Christ, Body of See *Body of Christ.*

Christ-Consciousness The consciousness of God which we feel Jesus must have had.

Christ Mind The action of thought from the highest motive.

Christ Principle inherent in us Christ, or the Universal Sonship, is the Reality of every person. We neither create nor sustain this Reality; it may only become revealed. Christ means the manifestation of God in us as us, the Universal Sonship; hence this Christ is right within us and needs but to be recognized and unified with.

Christ salvation A new and higher experience which comes from the recognition of the Indwelling Christ.

Christ the Incarnation of God Every man is an incarnation of God; anyone who recognizes this and lives in conscious and harmonious union with Spirit automatically becomes Christ.

Christian, scientific See *scientific Christian.*

Christ's second coming The dawning in the individual consciousness of the meaning of the teachings of Jesus. (See *coming, second.*)

circle From the standpoint of mental treatment it means that everything moves in circles; all thoughts complete themselves. Symbolic of the All-Embracing Principle without beginning or end.

Circle of Life The circle is a symbol, representing the Infinite, the First Great Cause before It moves into manifest form. The Circle of Life represents, in its downward arc, the coming of Spirit into matter, and, in its upward sweep, man's journey from gross materiality into pure Spirit, his perfected state.

circulation, spiritual equivalent of Realization of the Life Principle flowing through one with perfect freedom.

circulation, spiritual sense of Inner awareness that pure Spirit flows through one's entire being. This is the symbolic blood represented by "Emmanuel's veins." *Emman-*

uel means ''God with us.'' Spiritual circulation, then, is the recognition of God with us flowing through us.

circumstances, treatment must be independent of See *treatment must be.*

Co-Eternal The uncreated and always existing Truth.

Co-Existent That which exists with.

collective negative suggestions The entire thought of the race acting through any avenue of unbelief.

collective psychology Deals with the activities of groups or units.

Comforter—"It is expedient for you that I go away, for if I go not away the Comforter will not come unto you" This refers to the necessity of every man awakening within himself to Himself. The only final Saviour or Comforter is the Truth.

coming, second A teaching in the Christian Bible, referring to the Second Coming of Christ (Acts 1:11). We understand this to mean the development of the Christ Principle in man, which is the Principle of Divine Love-Wisdom, illumination, rather than the rebirth in form of the man Jesus.

communion See *prayer as a unifying; realization of; spiritual communion.*

communion with illusion Thinking only in reference to appearances viewed as separate from Cause. This is hypnotic and produces limitation.

communion with Reality Thinking in reference to the Truth as Wholeness, Beauty, Power, etc. This produces freedom.

Compensation, Law of That Principle through which one receives the equivalent for that which one has expended.

The Law of Cause and Effect operates through this Law of Compensation to supply the equal of that which has been given. It is a vehicle for the Divine Circuit of Life and is linked up with the law of giving and receiving. As we give full expression to Life, in the giving of ourselves, so Life returns to us in pouring forth Its gifts to us through various channels. Those who give grudgingly receive in small measure, and those who give generously receive richly.

complex A group of emotionally charged ideas around a central idea, partly or wholly buried in the subconscious, which exert an unconscious influence on one's behavior —that is, on one's thoughts, feelings, and actions.

concentration To focalize the attention on a single point. To keep the thought fixed, or centralized, by an act of will, on a certain idea. Having nothing whatever to do with any attempt to concentrate force, energy, power, mind, God, law, or anything else; having nothing whatsoever to do with influencing persons, places, or things; having no relationship to coercion, personal influence, hypnotism, mesmerism, or mental suggestion. From our viewpoint, concentration merely means engaged in thinking upon a certain idea.

conception The power in man of forming abstract ideas. The image or idea of anything formed in mind.

condition Any objective fact.

condition, transcend the See *transcend.*

condition, transpose the physical See *transpose.*

conditions See *mental treatment which; outward.*

conditions are reactions and not causes All causation is in the invisible realm of Mind; all conditions are effects reflected from these causes.

conditions—attracting those which are not in our conscious thought We always tend to attract that which is subjectively believed in whether or not we are conscious of it. In this way we are more or less controlled by race belief.

conditions, causes and See *causes.*

conditions, discordant See *separate.*

conscious intelligence Intelligence operating at the level of reflective or self-knowing consciousness.

conscious, treatment is See *treatment is conscious.*

consciousness The perception of existence. (See *Divine Consciousness.*)

consciousness and God are identical Consciousness means awareness; God is infinite awareness everywhere present in His entirety.

consciousness and intelligence manifest as created form Consciousness refers to awareness, and intelligence to the ability of awareness to make itself manifest. Form or creation is the manifestation.

consciousness changes the body with the change of thought Refers to the forming of new thought patterns, which automatically seek objective manifestation.

consciousness, changing the Refers particularly to rearranging subjective thought patterns. These subjective thought patterns automatically attract or repel whether we are asleep or awake.

consciousness, closet of That place in one's own mind where he works alone within himself and with Reality.

consciousness, disciplining See *disciplining consciousness.*

consciousness externalizes at its own level as water reaches its own level Just as water reaches its own level by its own weight, so our interior awareness, by the very act of being aware, objectifies itself or demonstrates conditions which are identical with such interior awareness or mental embodiment.

consciousness (my) is God See *my consciousness.*

Consciousness, Law of See *Law of Consciousness.*

consciousness, lifting up the Elevating the interior awareness to the perception of God, Good, Power, etc.

consciousness—movement of consciousness upon itself The inner action of intelligence can only be upon itself. This is the Law of Mind in action. (See *movement of consciousness; movement of Spirit.*)

consciousness must be conscious of something It is impossible to conceive of consciousness independent of an act of being conscious. It is impossible to be conscious without being conscious of something. In applying this principle to mental treatment, it means that treatment is always definite, conscious, and specific.

consciousness of Reality Both intellectual and inner awareness that the Divine Creative Spirit is within as well as without; Its immediate accessibility and usability.

consciousness, stream(s) of See *stream(s).*

consciousness, subliminal See *subliminal consciousness.*

consciousness, to enlarge the Deliberately and definitely to develop a greater expectancy of good and a deeper realization of life; to increase the spiritual imagination; to enlarge the acceptance of life; etc.

consciousness, understanding God at our level of See *understanding God.*

"Consider the lilies" The reference which Jesus made to nature, and his claim that the mental and spiritual world reproduces the physical on a higher level. That is, that all physical laws have corresponding mental and spiritual laws.

constant communion That which we continuously think, consciously or unconsciously, constitutes our communion with the universe.

contagion of thought Mob psychology; propaganda psychology; the tendency to believe what others believe, whether or not it be correct.

contemplation Entering into and becoming an embodiment of an idea realized through meditation.

contemplation, Spirit creates through Contemplation means inner awareness. Spirit creates by thinking within Itself, since, being All, It could not think outside Itself. This same Spirit within us creates through our contemplation; thus we reproduce the Universal on the scale of the individual.

continue in faith To meditate, pray, or treat, seeking continually a realization of faith, belief, acceptance, until the entire consciousness responds, following which demonstration takes place.

conviction, combine with definite intention Conviction alone is not enough; we are already convinced that God is good. Now we must have a definite intention running through our conviction, thus specializing the Law for particular purposes. We must say, "Because God is good, good is in this particular experience which I have right now."

Correspondence, Law of "As above, so below." Whatever the cause that sets the Law in motion, the result will have a corresponding relationship. It will be "tuned" to the same rate of vibration, so to speak. The thought that is in harmony with the Law of Good will reflect in harmonious relationships in the environment, or vice versa.

correspondent(s)   See *Law of Correspondents; Polarity.*

cosmic conception   Refers to the theory that the universal creative Spirit, operating through Its own Mind, gives birth to form.

cosmic consciousness   Consciousness of one's union with the Whole.

Cosmic Mind   The Universal Mind manifesting Itself as the cosmos.

cosmic purpose   Refers to the Divine Nature executing Its inevitable tendencies toward goodness, love, beauty, etc.

Cosmos   The entire manifestation of Spirit.

"could not enter in because of unbelief"   Nothing exists for the individual external to his consciousness of it; as faith brings about a constructive experience, so fear blocks our path.

creation   To bring into being by an act of thought. The ability to conceive of a thing is the creative power that brings it into manifestation. Creation is the movement of Mind upon Itself. (See *reality back of all.*)

creation the play of Life upon Itself   The Creative Principle makes things out of Itself by Itself becoming the thing that It makes. This is the action of a limitless Imagination upon an Infinite Law.

creative factor within us   Refers to the subjective law of our being.

Creative Law is always available   Since the Creative Law is not only around us but also at the very center of our being, It is, of a necessity, at the very center of our thought processes.

Creative Law is always neutral The Law of Itself knows neither good, bad, big, little, right, wrong, etc. It is always neutral. (We must never confuse the Law of Cause and Effect with the Spirit.)

Creative Medium Refers to the Law of Mind; the World Soul.

Creative Medium of Mind The universal Law of Cause and Effect. The subjective field which operates upon thought or upon which thought operates to produce conditions. The automatic, mental principle underlying the power of thought.

Creative Power is always receptive The very essence of the subjective life is its receptivity. The very fact that it is subjective compels it to receive images of thought.

creative process The creative process is an action of Mind upon Itself, whether it be the great Universal Mind, as God, creating a universe, or the action of Mind in man in his individual use of It. True creation is the unfoldment of an idea, the very urge of the Life Principle, as an Idea, to create something new out of apparently nothing. This may be illustrated by a musician working out a musical composition, an artist painting a picture, or an inventor conceiving of a new object for the use of mankind, etc. The original impulse is in feeling, which develops into action through ideation. As the idea unfolds in Mind, everything necessary to its perfect fulfillment is created with it, or is a part of its unfoldment.

creative series—the end of one is the beginning of another Esoteric term signifying perpetual evolution and expansion.

Creator and created are one   Creation is the passing of Being into becoming; the flowing of the Invisible into the visible. The Invisible does not change Its nature because It takes on form. The effect is Spirit, the Cause, taking the form of any particular effect.

creators with God   There is One Mind and we all use It, hence thought is creative.

"crooked (the) shall be made straight and the rough places plain"   A spiritual treatment has the power to straighten out any condition.

cross   A universal sacred symbol that has been used the world over, throughout the ages, from as far back as the human mind has been able to penetrate. Its four arms point to the four cardinal points, and the central point represents Deity, which flows out into humanity AS humanity. The perpendicular line may represent the positive, male Ray, or Spirit; the horizontal line, matter, the female principle, or soul.

The cross is not a purely Christian symbol, for it has been used in various forms in ancient Egypt, Chaldea, Greece, India (by the Brahmans and Buddhists), and in Judea by the Jews long before Jesus appeared on earth. Man is the very cross itself, as he stands with outstretched arms—Spirit ''crucified'' in matter, or caught up in form. Man descends from the Cross when he comes into true liberation through his understanding of his real Be-ing.

D

death   See *what; ''Whatsoever ye shall.''*

declare for the spiritual idea   That is, in mental treatment to affirm, for example, that the bloodstream represents the circulation of perfect Life, eliminating everything which does not belong to Wholeness.

declare that your treatment is law Mentally to realize that the Law of Life operating through your words is absolute.

decree Has no reference to personal will, influence, or compulsion, but refers to the act of self-choice in definitely setting a law in motion for some specific purpose.

decree a thing To announce a desire as an accomplished fact; to establish in thought; to declare in mind; to affirm; to believe; to know; to accept.

decree of human opinion What the majority of people believe in tends to take place in everyone's experience.

deep stillness of the soul The inner mental calm which follows a complete turning from objective confusion to the indwelling Spirit.

Deity, inward The Spirit within us.

deliberately changing our position in the Law Consciously building up new thought patterns which automatically reflect themselves as new conditions. (See *changing our position.*)

"Delight in the Law of the Lord" The laws of the universe produce beauty as well as utility.

demand upon the Universe Conscious and definite acceptance of some particular good.

demonstrate, enlarging our capacity to Dwelling on the idea of truth, goodness, beauty, love, wisdom, power, substance, or anything that is universal in its nature, until through an increase in our consciousness we are able to reflect a greater expectancy or receptivity into the Law of Mind.

demonstrating the Truth To produce a definite objective change in the physical body or in the body of one's affairs, as a result of consciously using the invisible Power of Mind and Spirit. (See *Truth known.*)

demonstration Any objective manifestation which takes place as a result of conscious inner awareness. (See *prayers; Truth known.*)

denial In working metaphysically for spiritual healing of the physical body, or for the healing of conditions, the denial of the reality of the undesired condition is used to help dissipate the negative idea that there can be any reality back of such a condition that could perpetuate it. Denial is a process of building up one's faith in the One Reality, perfect Good, by denying the existence, in Principle, of the apparent evil. Denial has its use in mental treatment, where argument is used in dissolving the condition, but is not needed as the student reaches the higher plane of thought, which is the true Spiritual Realm of Reality Itself, above the plane of so-called illusion where exist the pairs of opposites. Here there can be only affirmation, as the Eternal Perfection, which is ALL in all, is perceived.

denial in mental treatment Affirming that there is no opposite to good, God, and that what ought not to be has no real being.

denial—the practitioner never denies body The practitioner affirms that the body is an activity of right ideas; it is really universal and perfect.

denying evil Any mental statement, which, in affirming the supremacy of good, denies the reality of any opposite to good.

descending arc of the circle A term used to symbolize the descent of Spirit into matter, as material form. In man it symbolizes his incarnation in the physical universe.

The idea is Spirit functioning in and as gross materiality, which is a part of the experience of Life Itself. (See
ascending arc of the circle.)

descent of Spirit Means the passing of Spirit into form.

"desert (the) shall rejoice" The most commonplace things
in life and the waste places of human experience are converted into the Garden of God.

desire Irresistible urge toward self-expression. (See *"Whatsoever things."*)

despise not the day of small beginnings In making demonstrations we should be grateful for small results at the
beginning, provided there is a tendency in the right direction; we must learn by doing.

destroying error Either by a denial of a false belief or an affirmation of its opposite, which is the Truth, we erase the
effect of a false conclusion or straighten out a mistake in
mind. To destroy error means mentally to perceive that
it is neither person, place, nor thing; it is neither cause,
medium, nor effect. In mental treatment, the argument
of truth which denies and thus obliterates its apparent
opposite.

destructive power not in the universe The universe is one
indivisible Wholeness; if there were any final ultimate or
real element of destruction within this One, everything
would cease to function. All apparent destruction is but
a temporary derangement of thought processes which
produce such action.

determinism (metaphysical definition) The doctrine that the
will is not free, but is inevitably and invincibly determined by physical and psychical conditions.

Deva Angel, or Shining One. In Eastern philosophies, a
Stream of Life separate from humanity.

devil Anything which denies the unity of good, the allness of Truth, or our oneness with Spirit.

diagnosis, mental To uncover or bring to light and to correct any and all thoughts which contradict the Divine Presence as complete and perfect. (See *mental diagnosis*.)

difference between God and man is not in essence but in degree The Mind Power of the universe is in everyone, and it is the same Creative Genius which projects everything. Our mind is this Mind functioning at the level of our realization of life. As much of It as we use, that much of It we become.

differentiation That quality known as individuality in persons and things. It is a splitting up of the One Originating Spirit as It manifests in form. Differentiation is that which makes one unit of life different from every other unit, from the atom to an archangel, and beyond.

directing power The starting of any manifestation, from the creation of a solar system to man's smallest creative impulse, is in the word he speaks, which clothes his thought in form. "In the beginning was the Word . . . and the Word was God."

directing your treatment Stating what or who your treatment is for. Treatment should always be directed.

discarnate spirits Refers to the continuation of the ego after death; the continuation of the individual entity or stream of consciousness after physical death.

discipline of truth The will and the willingness to think in accord with the nature of our True Being.

disciplining consciousness Bringing our mental reactions under control; not holding thoughts, but rather consciously deciding what thoughts shall be loosed.

disease Lack of manifestation of health, or belief in such a lack.

disease as a claim, a belief, a supposition In spiritual mind healing, any discord is treated as though it were neither person, place, nor thing; it is treated as though it were merely a representation of false thought.

disease—destroy belief that it must operate Healing the thought of the belief that disease is either person, place, or thing, or that it has any channel for operation.

displace evil with truth For every belief in an opposite to good, provide a realization which affirms the presence of good.

dissolve your troubles In mental treatment we seek consciously to become aware that since God is All there is, negation has no real existence; in thought we seek to dissolve it into its native nothingness.

Divine Consciousness God-perception.

Divine Forgiveness Neither the consciousness of Spirit nor the laws of the universe hold anything against us; wherever we turn to them in recognition and acceptance, they immediately flow through us, imparting the Divine Givingness into our experience.

Divine Freedom See *personal choice.*

Divine Givingness The outpouring of Life in everything, on everything, and through everything.

Divine Incarnation Christ in us. The Spirit of God in man as man.

Divine Influx The surge of Spirit into self-expression through all people.

Divine Inheritance Every man inherits the entire kingdom of good; ''All that the Father hath is thine.''

Divine Law While embodying all laws, this phrase refers particularly to the Spiritual Cause and Effect. (See *obedience*.)

Divine Love The Spirit is forever imparting Its life to us; the complete givingness of Spirit.

Divine Mind A consciousness of Wholeness.

Divine Mother Symbol of the feminine or receptive aspect of the Creative Principle.

Divine Nature The true nature of all things. (See *"Thy will"; Will of God; "Ye ask."*)

Divine Plan Refers to the nature of the Divine Being; that is, if God is Love, then the Divine Plan is Love. The inevitable necessity that the Creative Spirit shall project Its own Nature into experience in order that It may know Itself.

Divine Potential That Spark of the Divine Flame of Life, within us, through which we may develop into a perfected human being—the Christ man, or the illumined one. The God-in-us that is mighty to do for us all that we can conceive ourselves to be. Through this infinite Potentiality for Perfection, in us, all things are possible.

Divine Principle Spiritual causation operating through Universal Law.

Divine Reality The truth about God.

Divine Science* An orderly and organized arrangement of the facts known about mental and spiritual law. The same as Spiritual Science.

Divine Urge The incessant demand toward self-expression. Psychologically referred to as the Id.

---

*Used as a generic, and not in reference to the Divine Science movement and teaching.—*Ed.*

doctrine and dogma Ecclesiastical beliefs; a definite tenet; a code of such tenets.

Doctrine—"If any man shall do His will he will know of the Doctrine" This has reference to the proof or demonstration of the Creative Principle; when we comply with It, It always manifests in our experience.

door—"I am the door of the sheep" *Sheep* refers to the Spiritual Principle in man, and *door*, like gate, to the entrance of this Spiritual Principle into salvation through a recognition of the "I Am."

doorway of opportunity always open New creation is eternally taking place uninhibited by ancient causation.

"Draw nigh unto God and He will draw nigh unto thee" The Principle responds to us by corresponding with our mental attitudes.

dream state Any belief which denies our unity with good.

drop the burden of the intellect There is nothing wrong with the intellect itself, but it is burden when it acts independently of a belief in a higher source of power.

duality A belief in more than one power back of things. Theologically, a belief in God and a devil. In philosophy, any belief that unity and multiplicity produce division. In Science of Mind, any belief that good has an opposite, such as good and evil, heaven and hell, etc. (See *Oneness can; philosophic.*)

duality—to affirm the truth and deny the negative does not mean that we practice duality An affirmation of Truth and a denial of its opposite are the same thing, since each affirms the supremacy of the good. We never deal with duality but merely with the dual use of Unity.

E

Eden This term is sometimes used to symbolize the Garden of the Soul, where man works in the creative soil of Mind to produce the perfect blossoms of perfected being. The Garden of Eden also signifies the Cradle of the human race on earth, where man began to develop human consciousness. The time of this dawn of consciousness is placed in the Mesozoic Age, which may be a reason for the Biblical story of the Serpent in the Garden—it being the Age of Reptiles.

effect See *Cause and Effect; Law of Cause and Effect; nothing but; Spirit is the realm; Truth is both.*

Ego From the spiritual viewpoint, the Real and eternal man.

elimination See *assimilation and elimination; mind as a law.*

embodiment See *we cannot experience.*

Emmanuel God with us: the Christ in each one.

energy, vitalizing Stands for the spiritual flow of Life.

engine of the subjective mind Refers to the Law of Cause and Effect, which is dynamic, mathematical, and creative, but which needs an engineer (conscious direction).

"Enter ye in at the strait gate" *Gate* signifies the entrance of consciousness into the realm of harmony. It is strait and narrow, since it must reject everything which denies the Eternal Good.

entity (general definition) "A portion of Reality which contains Its identity." (Metaphysical) An ego which maintains an individualized relationship with the whole; a spirit; a soul; a person. An individualized stream of God-consciousness *in* man *as* man. A form which has individual existence. Sometimes thoughts, which have been so energized by sustained mental atention and strong feeling, acquire actual form and are referred to as thought forms or entities.

equivalent(s)   See *Law of Mental Equivalents; mental equivalent.*

error   Any mistaken conclusion; from our viewpoint, that which contradicts the spiritual Reality.

error, impersonalizing   See *impersonalizing error.*

error, to dissolve   Refers to the act of mental treatment wherein one seeks to become aware of perfection instead of imperfection. (See *destroying; handling error; Truth dissolves.*)

error, uncovering   See *uncovering.*

Esoteric and exoteric   The inner and outer teachings of spiritual truths.

essence of being   Means that "The Highest God and the innermost God are One God."

establishing Truth in consciousness   To change the inner thought patterns until they accept the ever-present and ever-available Spirit of Wholeness.

eternal verities   Refers to fundamental truths that cannot change, particularly to the idea that Love, Wisdom, Power, Beauty, etc., are universal qualities accessible to all people—they are always there and always may be called upon.

eternity   See *time and.*

eternity is here   We are now the sons of righteousness just as much as we ever shall be.

ether   A term used to designate Original Substance, which is everywhere present, permeating all space.

etheric body   The bridge of atomic matter between the emotional and physical bodies. It extends beyond the physical form and is the vehicle for finer vibrations than can be felt in the physical body.

etheric vibrations Vibratory waves of force, in various degrees of intensity. These vibrations are the connecting links between all planes of existence, visible and invisible.

"every plant of the field before it was on earth" This means that the idea comes before the form. The Word of Spirit, as Law, creates form. Form is the effect; the word is its cause.

"Everyone that asketh receiveth" Refers to the Law of Cause and Effect whereby each must receive the full measure of his own consciousness. We are always attracting or repelling according to our thought.

evil A term used to imply the opposite of good. Evil is not a thing in itself, but is an *absence* of what is felt to be good or pleasing, as darkness is an absence of light, or death an absence of life. The term is usually linked with the idea of negation or destruction, though these forces, in themselves, are not really "bad." What appears to be destruction at times is only a vehicle for change. The term is entirely relative. What might seem evil to one man might be seen as good by another.

evil, belief in See *belief in evil creates evil; personalizing.*

evil, destroying See *good, destroying.*

evil, dominion over The recognition of good through spiritual awareness automatically overcomes that which denies good.

evil, impersonal nature of Evil of itself is neither person, place, nor thing. The belief that two and two make five never alters the fact that two and two make only four.

The belief that two and two make five does not belong to anyone; it is merely operating through someone's ignorance.

evil neither person, place, nor thing That which denies good is not an entity; has no location in Spirit; does not belong to anyone and cannot operate through anyone's experience.

evil, no medium for the operation of A spiritual consciousness does not attract evil thought. Only when thought is tuned to evil does it reproduce it.

evil, no power in Two and two never make five; evil is never a thing in itself, hence it has no eternal law to support it.

evil, origin of See *origin.*

evil—overcoming evil with good See *overcoming.*

evil, resist not See *resist.*

evil spirits Discordant and chaotic thought patterns consciously retained which tend to influence the conscious faculties negatively.

evolution A gradual unfoldment or development. The progress of a race or a species from a lower form of existence into higher forms, in line with the Principle of Life, which is ultimate Perfection. This does not imply that there will ever be a stopping point, for it is the nature of Life to forever unfold into higher and higher expressions of being.

evolution—man's future evolution depends upon his cooperation with nature Proven by all advanced in any science; the laws of nature pre-exist our use of them but are never forced upon us.

"Except a man be born again he cannot see the Kingdom of God" Our mental vision must be shifted from effect to cause. We must be born into the realization that we are living in a spiritual universe.

"Except the Lord build the house" That which is not of the truth cannot be eternal; that which is opposed to the truth destroys itself.

"Except ye be as little children ye shall not enter into the Kingdom" We should have a child-like and intuitive belief in the eternal goodness.

"Except ye believe that I Am, ye shall perish" Refers to the necessity of recognizing the inner spiritual Principle without which recognition the outward or physical man is not sustained. Has no reference whatsover to hell, devil, punishment, etc.

exoteric See *Esoteric.*

experience interprets reality to us Each man's life is, at any time, a result of the sum total of all his thought processes, both conscious and subjective. The thought processes are the creator of his experience and continue his present contemplation of God. However, the processes of thought can be changed, hence the experience can be altered.

explanation is the healing power Explaining and realizing that all life is One, complete, perfect, and changeless.

external world is the reflection of our within The sum total of our subjective thought patterns automatically projects itself into our physical bodies and environments, thus, ''What man has as well as what he is, is the result of the subjective state of his thought.'' If this were not true, changed mental attitudes would have no effect.

F

faith A *certain* knowledge, founded only on a firm belief, that a thing is true. A recognition of, and a belief in, certain principles. Belief in the impossible from an objective viewpoint. Unconditioned acceptance that there is an invisible Intelligence which guides and an invisible Law which controls and the complete belief that It is now doing so in one's life.

faith—"According to your faith" The answer to prayer of the demonstration following treatment is an objective representation of an inner mental and spiritual embodiment.

faith, active Consciously applying faith for definite purposes.

faith and understanding As applied to spiritual law we either have faith that there is some power that will produce the desired result, or we have an understanding that the law we use must produce such a result.

faith—approaching the Spirit as a child With complete and implicit trust; with unqualified acceptance; simply, directly, spontaneously and, above all, without effort.

faith as a mustard seed Refers to the power of one single positive thought.

faith, asking in Asking with unqualified acceptance. An unqualified acceptance of our own prayers as being answered.

faith based on understanding Does not deny the power of faith but, affirming the unity of all life and the perfection of all causation, strengthens our faith through knowledge.

faith by logic and reason Conviction arrived at through analysis. Scientific certainty of demonstrable law arrived at through understanding.

faith cure See *metaphysical healing*.

faith, field of See *field*.

faith in God through intuition An unreasoned but not necessarily unreasonable conviction that there is a Supreme Intelligence responding to us; an unquestioning reliance upon good. The deep conviction that there is a Power and a Presence which not only can, but will, respond to us.

faith in one's fellowman A conviction that the average person is trustworthy, reliable, and friendly.

faith in oneself A complete conviction that one is able to meet any situation that may arise; perfect self-confidence.

faith is a thing of thought It is self-evident that faith is the movement of consciousness and perception, of expectance and interior awareness, hence it can be consciously generated.

faith is complete when the subconscious no longer denies our affirmation This means that our faith is complete when subjective thought patterns no longer deny it; when nothing in the memory or belief denies it. So long as there is anything within us which denies our word, the word could become effective only as a mental suggestion; but when the interior and unconscious processes of thought are straightened out, then the word of faith becomes power.

Faith, Law of See *Law of Faith*.

faith must be in something Faith itself is an abstract conviction; a generalized belief or a complete acceptance of good, truth, beauty, etc. If this faith is to demonstrate some particular good, it can do so only by applying itself to that good—that is, through conscious acceptance of such good.

faith must be subjective to be effective While there is

anything in us that denies what we affirm, we shall neutralize our own word.

faith—not necessary to deny a fact in order to have faith
All facts are included in the One Mind; we need not deny sickness or human suffering in order to alleviate them, but, disregarding the fact, we must affirm its opposite.

faith overcomes fear Having resolved things into thoughts, the spiritual mind practitioner knows that his faith in good completely erases the fear of evil.

faith, passive General acceptance of good without conscious application.

faith, prayer of See *prayer of.*

faith, shield of See *shield.*

faith—Substance takes form through faith As Mind must be Mind to *something*, we must not only have faith, we must have faith in *something*. Prayer, to be effective, is specialized as well as generalized.

faith—we walk by faith not by sight All causes are invisible; because of their effects we have faith in the causes even though we do not see them. (See *"we walk."*)

faithful in thought Persistent in holding steadfastly to healing currents of Love, Joy, and Prosperity thoughts.

false appearance Any manifestation which is not in harmony with spiritual truth; which denies the fundamental unity and perfection of Being. Any objective fact which denies the fundamental premise of the unity of Good.

false argument, recognition of Understanding the thought patterns we wish to change.

false belief Used in the sense of believing that there is some power opposed to good, some law other than Divine. (See *right ideas destroy.*)

false belief about body   Any belief that the body is separated from Mind or Spirit, or is anything other than the body of spiritual ideas.

false belief uncovered   Mentally sensing that which denies the supremacy of Good, and mentally affirming its opposite.

false growth   Any false appearance in the physical body. (See *false appearance; growth, false.*)

false humility   As there is but One God, there is but One Man; each one is a member of this Christ Principle, and no one should deny his sonship.

false revelations   See *revelations, false.*

false sense   Any belief which denies the Divine Presence, the Divine Perfection, and Perfect Love.

false (the)—translating the false into the true   See *translating.*

fasting from poverty   The mind should definitely turn from the contemplation of anything that limits; thus it abstains from continuing to create limited circumstances. (See *"This kind."*)

fate   A belief in some power outside the self controlling the self.

Father   See *Heavenly Father; "Who."*

Father (the) and the son   The Divine Creative Spirit, the Parent Mind, is the Father; the individualization of this Parent Mind in us is the son. The Eternal "I Am" is One wherever we find It; the difference is not in essence but in degree.

"Father (the) is greater than I"   Although Jesus affirmed "The Father and I are one," he, of course, also pointed out that no individual manifests the whole of the Godhead.

Father, Son, and Holy Ghost The Infinite Spirit as Self-Knowingness, the Creative Principle of Mind as Law, and manifestion as effect.

"Father (the) Who seeth in secret" The invisible Intelligence at the center of our own being and of all being.

Father's house—"In my Father's house are many mansions" Refers to ascending planes of consciousness; the eternal expansion, progressive evolution; the future state as one of development; etc.

fatted calf Symbol of Fruits of the Spirit brought by love and wisdom and presented to our conscious reunion with good.

fear Faith negatively applied. (See *faith overcomes; neutralize fear.*)

feminine principle The Universal Soul or medium of thought action.

feminine principle in nature Refers to the universal creative Principle of Mind.

field of faith A subjective mental atmosphere existing among any group of persons who have been exercising faith, belief, expectancy, and acceptance. A dynamic acceptance created by a group of people which tends to benefit anyone who enters it. A creative atmosphere of conviction.

"fiery darts of the wicked" The negative impulses which rise out of the race consciousness; our own fear and doubt; accusations of others which we accept; etc.

finding one's center Mentally to acknowledge, to seek, to accept, and to understand that the Supreme Spirit is at the center of one's life.

finite (the), we can expand See *we cannot contract.*

fire Symbolic in its higher aspect of the Spirit, and of Wisdom, Divine Love, and Divine Life. In its lower aspect, signifies desire; sometimes the lower emotion. Fire as purification signifies that which consumes error, purifies experience, and regenerates consciousness; the purifying of the lower nature by love and truth.

"first cast out the beam out of thine own eye" We cannot give others what we ourselves do not possess.

First Cause God—Spirit—That from which all things come.

First Principle Universal Mind, or Spirit. The God Principle. Everything manifest has sprung from this Principle, as Divine Idea.

food A symbol of Reality and of Truth. The Reality which is to become assimilated.

food for thought A symbol of Wisdom, Truth, and Love, sustaining the soul.

"For as the Father hath life in himself so hath he given it to the Son to have life in himself" Man's life is the Life of God; there is but One Mind or Spirit from which man can derive life, intelligence, or power.

"For the invisible things . . . are clearly seen, being understood by the things that are made" This means that we go from the known to the unknown, that there are parallel laws, that every objective and visible fact has a subjective and invisible cause. If we study the fact, we shall understand the nature of its cause.

force In metaphysical parlance, force means the power or energy which man uses, or distributes. The term is used to designate the vibratory action of certain abstract principles, such as the Love Force, the Dark Forces, the Forces of Light, etc.

"Forgive and you shall be forgiven" The consciousness of sin in another is the consciousness of sin in one's own being. We are free from condemnation only as we no longer condemn.

"forgive us our debts as we forgive our debtors" The Law of Cause and Effect can only forgive as we ourselves first have forgiven. (See *"when ye."*)

forgiveness See *Divine Forgiveness; "Thy sins."*

form The world of form is the physical world about us. Anything that has definite shape, size, etc., has form. The specific qualities that make a thing what it is lend shape to its form. It is that distinctive quality that makes one thing appear as separate from another. It is a law that two forms of the same rate of vibration and manifesting on the same plane cannot occupy the same space at the same time. (See *Spirit is the realm.*)

Fountain of Life The Great Current of Life that forever flows through man which is the Eternal Spirit of God in him, a part of the Divine Circuit of Being. It is like a fountain at the center of man's being, forever flowing, which supplies his every need. To contact it he must center his attention within himself, attuning his thought to the Divine Source of his Life. As he does this, this Fountain of Power radiates Its Harmony and Strength all about him, as the Life within him and around him.

freedom The necessary prerogative of self-choice acting as a law of cause and effect, carrying with it the liabilities of its selectivity. (See *limitation and freedom; personal choice.*)

freedom under law There is nothing chaotic about the Law of Mind and Spirit; it is freedom *through* law, not *from* law.

freedom—"Within Thy Law is freedom" Since the Law of the Lord must be perfect and limitless, it must be freedom.

functions as spiritual ideas See *organs.*

G

Garden of Eden　Refers to the garden of the soul. (See *serpent in.*)

Generic Law　The principle that everything is created according to its type or species, or class. The seed atom that makes anything what it is and not something else, be it man or flower or animal. The generic law deals with groups rather than individuals.

"Get thee behind me, Satan"　Let all thoughts of fear, doubt, uncertainty, and evil depart from me.

"Give and to you shall be given"　Refers to the Law of Cause and Effect as immutable and mathematical.

Giving and Receiving, Law of　This is the principle of the Divine Circuit of Life. Life flows out from the Absolute, through man, or form—and returns to its Source. When man tries to hold his good, he blocks his channel for receiving more good. Those who give of themselves the most, receive the most, unless they block the circuit again in the attitude that they wish only to give. In this case they are apt to impoverish themselves. Life is a giving of Itself in abundance. Nature gives of herself freely, for the sheer joy of expression. The bird pours forth its song as its expression of life. The rose exhales its fragrance, and all who pass may enjoy it. The important point is to give as an expression of abundant living, not with the idea of getting back in full measure. The Divine Circuit takes care of the return, and man needs only to be receptive to his good.

giving is not complete without receiving　Even though the gift of life is made, its circuit is not complete until we have received it. Hence, ''to as many as believed gave He the Power.''

God Deity: The Supreme Being, the Absolute, Eternal, Infinite. Spirit, Reality, or Truth in its absolute sense. (See *consciousness and God are identical; in God; knowing God; knowledge of; my consciousness; personalness; pleasing.*)

God and Man—difference is in degree and not in essence
Since there is but One Life, the Life of man is God in man as man. The difference is not in the nature of this Reality but in the amount of It which flows through consciousness. (See *difference; Perfection.*)

God and the manifestation of God as person must be One
If Reality were separate from us, then we could never recognize anything. But because Reality is within us, we recognize other things which also are within Reality.

God appears through idea Spirit being infinite Mind, Its activity consists of limitless idea. It is only through the manifestation of idea that we become conscious that Spirit is Mind.

God as a Living Presence The dynamic presence of the Universal Spirit, permeating everything and forever making Itself known.

God as Life Spirit is the very essence, the very livingness of everything; the animating Principle in everything which makes everything what it is.

God as Love The entire nature of the Divine Spirit is to forever give Itself to Its creation.

God as self-active Spirit Spirit is both impulsion and energy; It is at the same time designer and designed. There is no outside to Spirit. All inspiration derives within it. It is in us, therefore the ability to live or to express life is not something derived from an external source, but is already inherent within our own natures.

God bless you The recognition of the Divine Presence as

protection, guidance, and peace. Therefore to bless a thing is to protect it.

God, Body of See *Body of God.*

God-Conscious(ness) See *becoming God-conscious; center of God-Consciousness; God is our; man as a center.*

God—faith in God through intuition See *faith in God.*

God, Grace of Symbolizes the higher nature, which raises the lower into a consciousness of God.

God in me The Originating Creative Principle is at the center of my life. (See *"My Lord."*)

God Incarnate The Presence of God in man as man.

God in the still small voice All processes of nature are quiet. The unfolding rosebud silently proclaims a dynamic power expressing the beauty inherent in Reality.

God in us knowing Himself Since there is but One Mind, that Mind in us is God in us. It can be nothing else. And since this Mind can know nothing outside Itself, the operation of this Mind through us as thought is the announcement of the Infinite to Itself. This is why thought is creative. Not by willing, wishing, coercing, or concentrating, but merely because it is its nature to be creative.

God is an impartial giver The Infinite has no preferences; It is both impartial and impersonal, giving alike to each and to all. Thus it is written that to as many as received, gave He the power.

"God is not a God of the dead, but of the living" The Principle of Life can never conceive death; that which has real self-conscious life lives forever.

God is our very self Since there is only One Mind, Spirit, or Life Principle from which anything can be formed, then there is but one final Self personified in innumerable centers within this Self. Every man is a center of God-Consciousness. There is One Self back of all people.

God is Spirit God is the Eternal Presence within, around, and through everything. They that worship Him must worship Him in Spirit and in Truth—that is, in accord with the Truth about His nature.

God, man reveals See *man reveals.*

God, my consciousness is See *my consciousness.*

God, Nature forever unfolding See *Nature of God.*

God, no life separated from See *no life.*

God no respecter of persons Just as the Infinite knows neither big nor little, It knows neither good, better, nor best. There can be no Infinite Intelligence which recognizes one person as having more merit than another.

God-Power, science of See *science of God.*

God-Self, the The Real Spirit Divine; the Christ in us. The reality of every man is God; man is an individualized center of this indivisible God Consciousness.

God, talking to See *talking.*

God the Healer The recognition that it is not personal will-power, mental suggestion, or persuasion, but the Divine Creative Principle acting with mathematical accuracy.

God—"The highest God and the innermost God is One God" Since there is but One Life Essence, the spiritual Intelligence within us is the same Intelligence within all things, and the same Intelligence that governs everything.

God the Knower and God the known Image and reflection are but two ends of the same thing.

God the Knower—the act of knowing and the thing known
Spirit is Cause, medium, and effect; essence, law, and order; involution and evolution; unmanifest mechanical processes and manifestation.

God—turning to God in thought See *turning to.*

God—understanding God at the level of our consciousness
See *understanding God.*

God, unifying with See *unifying.*

God, Will of See *Will of.*

God within us This does not mean that God is located in or limited to our within, but that since the Divine Mind is omnipresent, It must be in, as well as around, us. Hence, it is written that "The highest God and the innermost God is One God."

God, Word of See *Word of God.*

God works for us through us As any energy must take the form of the instrument through which it flows, so Spiritual Power, to be effective in our experience, must first operate through our mental acceptance.

God, you are See *you are God.*

God's Ideas, omnipresence of All qualities of Spirit are ever present; Truth and Beauty exist everywhere, and wherever recognized immediately spring into manifestation.

God's Kingdom a government of law There are laws in the mental and spiritual world which govern all actions and all reactions, just as they do in the physical. The mental and spiritual is but a reproduction of the physical on a higher level.

God's Presence Like the ethers of physics, the Spirit of God is in everything, through everything, and around everything; since Spirit is the very essence of intelligence, there is a mind quality in everything which responds to our recognition of It.

God's workshop The Mind, which uses tools of thought.

Good The Reality, of which evil is but an apparent and transitory opposite.

good, actively conscious of It is not enough merely to say that good is. This is passive consciousness. Such statements should be followed by declaring that ''this good is operating in my experience now.''

good, destroying evil with a consciousness of As light dissipates darkness; as a change of temperature melts the solid form of water, which is ice; so a consciousness of Good dissipates not only the consciousness of evil, but its manifestation.

good, immediate availability of Since the laws of the universe never change, and since the Divine is forever present, then good is where we see it.

Good, tuning into See *tuning into Good.*

good will endure, evil must perish by its own self-destruction Suffering and punishment inevitably follow the wrong use of the Laws of Life, whether this wrong use is done in ignorance or with malicious intent. The universe is just, because it is always in perfect equilibrium.

Gospel—"The God-Spell" The good news of the Kingdom of Heaven; the proclamation of the Omnipresence of Good.

"Government (the) shall be upon his shoulders" The Law of Mind is self-executing; the universe is self-existent.

Grace See *God, Grace of.*

growth, false A wrong arrangement of cell life in the physical body. Translated into terms of mind, the Spirit never misplaces anything. The Truth of Being is harmonious as well as representative of the Divine Harmony, which is always in perfect arrangement, etc. (See *false growth.*)

growth in understanding An ever-increasing realization of the Spiritual Universe and of our union with It and with Its laws.

Growth, Law of See *Law of Growth.*

guru A spiritual teacher. An Indian term meaning, literally, "a dispeller of darkness."

H

habit as a subjective activity Subjective thought patterns tend always to objectify themselves under given conditions and situations; being subjective thought activities, habits can be removed through mental treatment.

Hades The underworld. Drama of the soul in its conflict with opposing desires. State of consciousness before the transition from the lower to the higher plane of perception. (See *Hell.*)

"hairs of your head are numbered" has reference to the All-Knowing Mind, in which all facts are contained in One Unitary Wholeness, ever available to the thought of man.

handling a belief Refers to the action of thought which governs, understands, and explains the essential nothingness of any opposite to good.

handling error Refers to any statement in consciousness which denies the reality of that which appears to be an opposite to good.

harmony exists irrespective of our experience Nothing that we think changes Reality; it merely changes our relationship to It. (See *unity necessitates.*)

"He hath broken the gates of brass and cut the bars of iron" There is no solid to the Spirit; no opposition; no adversity.

"He . . . sendeth His rain on the just and the unjust" The Divine Creative Spirit knows nothing of goodness or badness any more than It knows big or little; It gives of Itself alike to each and all because this is Its nature. However, each one, being an individual, uses this Divine beneficence in his own way; thus individually he may bring what he calls good or evil upon himself.

"He that diggeth a pit shall fall into it" We cannot be separated from our own consciousness; the evil we would do is done unto us.

"He that findeth his life shall lose it; and he that loseth his life for my sake shall find it" Whenever we discover a greater truth, the lesser vision slips away. We must lose the lesser as it merges into the greater.

Healer, God the See *God the Healer; practitioner.*

healing See *mental healing; spiritual healing; spiritual mind healing; theory; transpose; Truth is that; we heal.*

healing a sick business Mentally coming to see, and stating, that there is a Divine Activity in and through the business and the thought of everyone who conducts it.

healing agency, most powerful Realization of the Divine Presence as Love, Harmony, Wholeness, Action, Law, Order, etc. (See *spiritual communion as a.*)

healing as a mental problem The spiritual practitioner's work has nothing to do with time, place, condition, or person. He deals only with thought.

healing—metaphysical vs. faith cure See *metaphysical healing.*

healing, no responsibility in The practitioner's sole obligation is scientifically to know the Truth; the responsibility of Its action is solely in the realm of cause and effect. (See *personal responsibility.*)

healing, personal sense in It is not the person that heals, but the Principle operating through him.

healing—practitioner the first to be healed See *practitioner is.*

healing—psychic development not necessary See *psychic development.*

healing, realization is the See *realization is.*

healing, spiritual conception in See *spiritual conception.*

Heaven Harmony—Wholeness—Health—Physical Well-being—Happiness—Mental peace, poise, and well-being. (See *treasures.*)

Heaven and the new earth True spiritual vision interprets things more nearly as they are; the physical body and human experiences become regenerated through spiritual understanding.

Heavenly Father The Divine and Universal Creative Spirit immediately perceived as an indwelling Presence. The "Father which art in heaven" is the incarnation of God in us.

Hell—Hades—Sheol Symbolic of the lower plane of consciousness. The torment of experiencing that which contradicts Truth. The purification of desire, etc. (See *Hades.*)

here and now Reality in Its entirety is present with us at all times; in every moment in which we live; here and now.

heredity From the viewpoint of Science of Mind, the transmission of subjective tendencies.

higher and lower worlds Symbols of the ideal nature on the higher plane. The prototype of Reality and of the manifestation of Its nature on the physical plane.

higher self See *lower and.*

holding thoughts Refers to the mistaken idea that in spiritual mind practice we hold thoughts for people.

holding thoughts versus knowing the truth In spiritual mind treatment we do not hold thoughts, we do not concentrate. Demonstrations are not made by willing, mental coercion, or spiritual concentration, but rather through a silent recognition of the immutable Principle at work. We seek to recognize spiritual perfection in any situation, circumstance, etc. This correct recognition results in a right demonstration.

Holy Communion, sacrament of The symbolic representation of the continuous incarnation of God in man.

Holy Ghost Same meaning as Holy Spirit. (See *Father, Son; Holy Spirit.*)

Holy of Holies Represents the sanctuary of the heart or our innermost thought as it lifts itself toward the contemplation of Reality.

Holy Spirit The Universal Presence, in which we all live and which also manifests Itself through us. (See *Father, Son.*)

Holy Trinity Spirit as Absolute Intelligence; Mind as Law; form as manifestation.

human and Divine mind Human or limited way of thinking vs. a less limited way of thinking.

human consciousness Human perception.

human mind A consciousness of separation.

humility of self This does not mean self-depreciation; it means recognizing the greatness of the Whole; the purity of Spirit; the perfection of God, flowing through us, unobstructed by anything that is vicious or anything that sets us apart as being better than, or different from, other people.

husbandman Symbolizes the Spiritual Self as it tills the mental soil and brings forth a spiritual and perfect harvest.

husbandman of the Lord Biblical reference to man as one who uses the Divine gifts to bring forth the fruits of action.

hypnotic influence of negative thought The belief that there must be cycles of depression, war, pestilence, famine; the sum total of human negation, fear, sense of separation, etc.

hypnotized from the cradle to the grave Most people live under the law of mental suggestion or race belief, which acts as a mesmeric influence.

I

"I Am," the The "I Am" is both individual and universal: Individually it means the Life Principle within us; universally it means "The Thing Itself." In the universal It is God the Living Spirit Almighty; in the individual it is God the Living Spirit individualized. "I am that I Am" means God. (See *instinctive.*)

"I am the bread of life" The "I Am" in man is God or Truth. "The Truth is bread which refreshes our minds and fails not; changes the eater, and is not Itself changed into the eater." Bread is the symbol of spiritual food.

"I am the first and the last" Spirit is both Cause and Effect.

"I am the Lord and there is none else" There is only one Mind, one Power, and one Law running through all manifestation.

"I am the Lord . . . Beside me there is no saviour" Refers to the universal "I Am" operating through the individual I. Conscious use of this spiritual Power is our true Saviour.

"I am the vine, ye are the branches" There is one universal Christ Principle; we are all members of this perfect body.

"I can do all things through Christ" That is, in conscious union with the indwelling Spirit all things are possible.

"I can of mine own self do nothing" It is only through conscious cooperation with the Creative Principle that we can hope to draw the greatest power from It. Any energy shut off from its source soon becomes exhausted.

"I have blotted out . . . thy transgressions" A correct use of the Law transcends previous experiences.

"I have put my words in thy mouth" Man reproduces the universal Wholeness in his individual life.

"I judge no man" Judgment, punishment, and reward are in accord with the eternal Law of Cause and Effect; there is no superior intelligence that sits in constant judgment over our acts.

"I set before you . . . a blessing and a curse" Refers to the neutral law of mind, which produces divergent experiences.

"I shall be satisfied when I awake with thy likeness" Nothing can satisfy us until we awake to the truth of our being.

"I will contend with them that contend with thee" Refers to the Law of Cause and Effect; whatever sets destructive causation in motion must finally be destroyed by it.

"I will remember their sins no more" In mental treatment the entire effect of past mistakes is wiped out.

"I will work, saith the Lord, and who shall hinder me?" There is one Power, which knows no opposites.

Id Psychological expression meaning "it." From a metaphysical viewpoint, the cosmic urge toward self-expression manifesting through the individual as the Libido.

Idea, Divine See *"whose."*

Idea, God appears through See *God appears.*

idea, man as mind instead of See *man as mind.*

idea (spiritual), supply as See *supply as.*

idea, true—replacing false belief with See *replacing.*

idea, universal See *universal idea.*

ideals—conduct is subconsciously conditioned by spiritual ideals All of our ideals tend to revolve around the idea of our relationship to the universe.

ideas See *word is.*

ideas are to the invisible what things are to the visible Ideas are actual Substance in mental form. The visible is the counterpart of ideas.

ideas, Mind can only operate upon See *Mind can.*

ideas of supply See *supply, ideas.*

ideas, organs as spiritual See *organs; physical organs.*

ideas, right See *right ideas.*

identification The principle that "like attracts like." In thought, one must identify himself with that which he would draw into his experience. To be successful, one must identify oneself with success, etc.

identity, spiritual See *spiritual identity.*

If God be for us, He cannot be against us Means that there is only one Power; the universe is a unity and not a duality. There is no evil to oppose the Truth.

"If our earthly house . . . were dissolved, we have a house . . . eternal in the Heavens" We have a spiritual body as well as a physical one.

"If the blind lead the blind, both shall fall into the ditch" We heal fear only by faith, lack only through the consciousness of abundance; we enter heaven only by deserting hell; etc.

ignorance of the Law excuses no one This, of course, is held to be true relative to all known laws. In dealing with the laws of mind, it means that they react to our thought whether we are conscious of the fact or not. Hence, the very law which could produce freedom may be producing bondage.

illumination A spiritual state of mind which follows the New Birth.

illumined consciousness Has the same meaning as Christ-Consciousness.

illusion Any mistaken idea about the Truth.

illusion—belief does not make it real, while knowledge of Reality dispels illusion We must assume that back of all human thinking there are eternal verities. Our thought does not create these verities, it merely interprets them. Hence, belief in illusion does not create real illusion, it merely misinterprets Reality—while an understanding of Reality does dissipate the belief in illusion.

illusion may be believed in, truth may be known We can only know that which is so; apparent knowledge of anything which is not so is an illusion. To assume that truth is an illusion would be to assume that the more truth one knows, the more bondage he must experience; but to understand truth as a Reality dispels the illusion of bondage. For example, when everyone believed that the world was flat, the real world remained round; however, the illusion of a flat world did limit the experience of those who believed in it.

image and likeness, His It is man's nature to be like God. Spiritual man is God in such a degree as his consciousness functions in harmony with a complete love of, and unity with, the One Creative Principle.

image, mental See *mental image.*

imagination and will Imagination is the power of the Word; will is its direction. (See *will as a directive.*)

immaculate conception All birth is immaculate since all life proceeds from one Source, which is pure Spirit.

immaterial Refers to the formless Substance of Spirit.

impersonal principle of mind The Law is no respecter of persons but works alike for each and all.

impersonal spiritual healing See *spiritual healing, impersonal.*

impersonalizing error To realize that it belongs to no person and is operating through no one, that it is not a thing in itself, but is merely a belief.

impersonalizing negation Realizing that negative conditions do not belong to anyone, have no basis for being, and cannot be believed in by anyone. They are never things in themselves. To realize that whatever the false claim may be, its exact opposite is the truth. It is a correct understanding of this which enables one to impersonalize both evil and its manifestation; it is neither person, place, nor thing; neither law, cause, medium, nor effect; it belongs to no one, finds entrance through no one's thought, and operates in no one.

"In Adam all die . . . in Christ shall all be made alive" A symbolic presentation of the lower and higher forms of consciousness. Adam represents the lower mind, or the intellect, isolated from Spirit; Christ represents the new birth.

in God and of God The Life Principle that is within man is the same Life Principle that is around him; he is both in It and of It.

"In quietness and in confidence shall be your strength" The greatest power comes from the most intense stillness.

incarnate spirit Any person living in the flesh.

incarnating God Power Becoming increasingly aware of the Divine Presence, Perfection, and Power.

Incarnation See *Divine Incarnation.*

individual identity in mind No two people are alike in Mind any more than they are in the physical world; all individual thought vibrations are unique to the one who creates them and belong to no one else. Each individual is a unique expression of God.

individual subjective mind is never an entity It is rather the sum total of thoughts, feelings, emotions, acquired and inherited, acting as an entity.

individual, Universal must become See *Universal must.*

individuality The unique individualization of God Consciousness at the center of conscious self-awareness. Pertaining to man, a unique individualization of the Universal

Spirit. No two individuals are exactly alike, yet all are rooted in one common unity. Behind each individuality is all of Reality. Individuality exists by virtue of necessity and, unlike personality, cannot be changed.

individuality must be spontaneous It would be impossible even for God to make a mechanical individual, since the very word implies self-choice and freedom; thus individuality must discover itself.

individualizing the Law of Cause and Effect The use that each individual makes of the Law of Mind causes a flow of Its creativeness into the form of such use.

individualizing the Universal Law Just as there is one Mind which we all use, so the universal Law of Mind is individualized where we use It. In this way the Universal works for the individual through the individual at the level of the individual's comprehension of It as working.

individuals in the mental and spiritual world Just as no two physical thumbprints are alike, thus demonstrating the uniqueness of individuality, so no two persons' minds or spirits are identical; for while there is but One Mind and Spirit, which we all use, each individualizes It in a unique way. Each personifies the Universal. Thus there is no sameness even in the Universe of Unity.

inertia of thought This has both a psychological and a metaphysical meaning. Habitual thought patterns appear to resist dislodgment. However, persistent affirmation and denial will uncover and bring to light any thought pattern.

Infinite Intelligence is omnipresent Because the Mind of the Universe is one indivisible unit, all of It is present wherever our attention is focused.

Infinite Person The Supreme Consciousness in the universe.

The Mind of God as Knowingness, Awareness. The limitless Personalness ever seeking expression through our personality.

Infinite, Sustaining See *Sustaining.*

inheritance See *Divine Inheritance.*

inherited tendencies Prenatal subjective influences. In its larger sense, the entire race experience subjectively incarnated in all human beings. The collective unconscious. The subjective thought contains family and racial characteristics and tendencies which are more or less transmitted to everyone.

inner Life: The true life in each of us. The deep Self within, which radiates through the mind as thought, through the physical form as action, through the emotions as feeling.

inner Light Light stands for the radiation of pure Spirit, casting its ray through man by incarnation. There is absolute Light as well as perfect Life at the center of everyone's being.

inner Saviour Consciousness of Truth and Unity.

inner teaching Refers to the spiritual philosophy which affirms the spiritual nature of man.

inner Voice Intuition guiding us; nothing supernatural. The laws of Mind and Spirit, like the laws of physics, are perfectly natural in their own realm, and when we understand them we can make conscious use of them.

insanity Fundamental error that the brain thinks, therefore, that if the brain becomes impaired, thinking stops. A belief that brain grooves create intelligence rather than that intelligence creates brain grooves. Spirit, being the only Intelligence, constitutes the only Mind. Man's mind demonstrates the perfect Intelligence of God. Mind is omnipresent, hence the active intelligence of Mind is functioning everywhere.

inspiration   From the human side, contact with the subconscious of an individual or race. From the spiritual viewpoint, contact with Universal Spirit.

instinctive omniscient "I Am"   The God within us which instinct and intuition feels, knows, and accepts.

intangible values   Values which, while they cannot be weighed nor measured, are yet real; such as Love, Truth, Beauty, etc. All values are intangible from the standpoint of being seen, since all causation is invisible. Love is an intangible value because it is something that cannot be weighed and measured by physical instruments.

integration   Mental wholeness; the putting together of all parts of the mind so that they function as one normal individual.

"integrity (the) of the upright shall guide them"   Refers to the Law of Cause and Effect.

intellect as the tool of the Spirit   All thought processes should be dominated by a realization of the omnipresence of good. The intellect is the directive agency, the Spirit is the creative power.

intellect, spiritualizing the   Bringing the conscious and logical processes of thought into conformity with the idea of Truth, Love, Beauty, etc. This in no way denies the intellect.

intellectual acceptance and spiritual realization   In mental treatment the practitioner makes intellectual statements; that is, his statements are definite, concise, conscious, and directive; in order to be meaningful they must become spiritual realizations; the two are combined.

intellectual and emotional faculties Intellectual faculties, like the will, are discriminating but not creative. It is the emotion of conviction, feeling, and belief which is creative.

intelligence That part of the mentality concerned with acquisition and retention of knowledge as distinguished from emotion and will. From the standpoint of universal law, it means mind in action: Creation flowing from the invisible into the visible, from cause to effect with mathematical precision, without personal self-consciousness. Spirit is both Infinite Intelligence and Infinite Consciousness. The Law of Mind in action used in mental treatment is intelligent but not volitional. The Law of Mind in action is a mechanical but intelligent reaction to the consciousness which sets it in motion.

intelligence, atomic See *atomic intelligence.*

Intelligence, Infinite See *Infinite Intelligence.*

Intelligence makes a demand on Itself The urge of Spirit to express, operating through Mind, productive of form.

intelligence, subconscious See *subconscious intelligence.*

Intelligence, Universal See *Universal Intelligence.*

intelligent Law The Law of Mind knows how to adapt means to ends; It knows how to project our affirmation into experience; It responds intelligently as well as creatively.

intention In working with mental law, definite intention is necessary in the receptive attitude of the student, as well as in his active processes. He must have a clear idea of what quality he desires to have fulfilled in him, and by his intent permit that quality to develop in him. (See *conviction.*)

interior awareness precedes evolution That something

back of the evolutionary push which experience did not put there. The primal urge toward self-expression.

intuition Inner awareness of spiritual truths without conscious process of thought. (See *faith in God.*)

intuitional realization Realization arrived at without processes of reasoning. Interior awareness without any argument.

inversion A wrong use of the Creative Power, in that the person seeks only the outer manifestation of the thing he wants in his life, instead of contemplating only the Divine Principle of Being, Which includes his good, his perfect freedom. Inversion is to reverse the proper order of a thing. Fear is an inversion of faith. In fear the Creative Law of Mind is used to tear down and destroy, which is an inversion of the principle which builds up. It is a negative or upside-down use of faith. It is a perpetuation of the old circle of limitation, rather than the use of the Creative Power to attain liberation from the law of necessity.

invisible supply The Creative Law of Spirit is ever waiting to be called into manifestation; that from which all conditions flow; the Substance back of all form; this Substance is the universal and abstract essence of all concrete supply. It is Supply in Its liquid form uncaught in any mental mold.

"Invisible things . . . being understood by the things that are made" We judge the unseen by the seen. There is always an invisible back of the visible. (See *"For the invisible"; visible.*)

invoking creative Power Just as a seed planted in the creative soil invokes the Law—that is, sets it in motion—so treatment invokes the Creative Law of Mind, sets It in motion.

invoking the Law Like planting a seed in the ground, which invokes the creative soil, so a mental treatment invokes the Law of Mind, or sets It in motion, for definite purposes of creating the condition specified in the treatment.

Isis Symbolizes the Creative Principle in nature.

isolation and loneliness, sense of Failing to understand that the Spirit is in all people and, being forever One with Itself, unifies all people.

"It is the Father's good pleasure to give you the Kingdom" We do not bargain with God; we learn to receive that which has already been given. We receive and give only in such degree as we enter into the nature of the giver.

"It is the Spirit that quickeneth" All external life is an effect. Most of our mental life is merely a repetition of thoughts already formed. True and original inspiration derives from the higher reaches of consciousness, which is spiritual or conscious oneness with God.

J

Jachin One of the two great pillars that stood at the entrance of the Temple of Solomon, referred to in the Bible and in other sacred writings. Jachin symbolizes the impersonal element of the Universe—the Law, the Great Universal Power. Unity. One. (See *Boaz.*)

Jacob wrestling with the angel Symbolizes the problem of existence and man's relationship to God, which must finally be met in every person's individual consciousness.

Jacob's ladder Symbolizes the upward pathway of the soul. The ascending angels represent an uplifted consciousness; the descending angels represent intuition.

Jesus as a revelation of the will of God　The life and teaching of Jesus illustrate the nature of Reality as Love, Wisdom, and Law. The Divine Nature and the Divine Will are One. (See *mind that was.*)

Jesus Christ as Saviour　This does not refer to Jesus Christ as a person, but to the Christ Principle in all people, which Jesus revealed. It refers to accepting his method and using it in our own personal lives.

Jesus washing the feet of the disciples　The Law serves us when we first obey Its nature.

journey of the soul　Refers to the theory that man's soul emanates from Perfection and travels on the road of experience in order that it may return to Perfection, individualized. Symbolized by the story of the Prodigal Son.

"Judge not according to appearances"　Since Absolute Spirit acting as immutable Law is the only causation, we are not to take our patterns of thought from any manifested form.

"Judge not that ye be not judged"　The same law by which we judge others, completing its cycle, judges us accordingly.

judgment and justice　Refers to the law of compensation, or cause and effect.

judgment of God's Law　The Law of Cause and Effect working. (See *"I judge."*)

K

Karmic Law　Mental cause and effect.

keeping the eye single　Holding thought steadfastly to truth.

Kingdom, the That place of complete peace, strength, and harmony that is found within, deep in the innermost Self of each. (See *"It is the Father's"; "Except a man"; "Except ye be."*)

"kingdom (a) divided against itself cannot stand" Evil does not combat good, merely because there are no ultimate dualities. The ultimate Principle of Life is one and undivided, else we should have chaos and not cosmos.

Kingdom of God Refers to the invisible essence of Reality, governing everything in accord with Divine and harmonious laws of Love, Wisdom, Truth, Beauty, and perfect manifestation. From the human viewpoint, the Kingdom of Heaven means a consciousness of harmony.

"Kingdom of God cometh not with observation" The Kingdom of God is an interior perception and not an external viewpoint. It is not external but inner. The Kingdom of God is within you.

"Kingdom of God is like leaven" Truth introduced into consciousness has the power to raise our whole mental outlook to a higher level. It leavens the lump of subjective error.

"Kingdom of Heaven is like a grain of mustard seed" As the very small mustard seed grows into a large plant, so our inward thoughts and desires, when in conformity with Truth, take form and become multiplied through the creative process of Mind.

Kingdom of Heaven likened to a child Refers to the consciousness of simplicity, trust, and confidence with which one should accept that the kingdom of good is at hand.

knock—"Behold I stand at the door and knock" The Eternal Reality is ever present around us. Truth always is, but can operate through us only as we recognize it.

Good is ever available. The Christ Principle awaits our recognition.

knowing God We know God only in so far as the Divine Attributes become personalized in our own experience. Therefore, to know virtue is to be virtue; to know truth is to become truth; to know peace is to embody peace; to know love is to personalize it.

knowing God through ideas We must judge the unknown by the known.

knowing the Truth Rearranging our thinking in order to affirm the Allness of Good, its ever-availability, and its omni-action in our affairs. To sense the Divine Creative Wisdom governing and the Divine Creative Law executing the Will of Wisdom, Truth, and Beauty in human affairs.

knowing the Truth and believing that which is not so We may believe that two and two make five, but we cannot know that two and two make five; we can only really know that two and two make four; hence, we may believe in an illusion, but we can never know that which is not so. We can only know the Truth.

knowing the Truth is the Saviour Salvation from pain, fear, etc., is arrived at through understanding the supremacy of Spirit.

knowing the Truth is treatment Mentally claiming the Allness of God; denying anything which contradicts this Allness; sensing the Spiritual Reality.

knowledge of God Systematic understanding of the nature of Reality.

knowledge, the only source of All knowledge must come through one, or another, of a combination of: science, which is a demonstrable knowledge of natural laws and causes; philosophy, which is an expression of opinion and may or may not be correct; and intuition, sometimes called revelation, which is a direct perception of truth without processes of conscious reasoning.

L

Law The invisible mechanics of the universe pertaining to Mind, to Spirit, or to physics. The Law of Mind in action used in mental treatment is intelligent but not volitional. The Law of Mind in action is a mechanical but intelligent reaction to the consciousness which sets it in motion. (See *Creative Law; Divine Law; Generic; intelligent; Karmic; Life Principle as Law; parallel; Spirit inspires; Spirit is form-giving; thought moves.*)

Law, the The basic Law of Life is the Law of Unity, of Wholeness.

law (the) and the word The creative power of mental law is set in motion by the word consciously spoken.

Law, changing our position in the See *changing our position in the Law.*

Law, definite use of We are either using the Law definitely or indefinitely, consciously or chaotically. Scientific practice consists in conscious application of thought for specific purposes.

law, freedom under See *freedom under; freedom—"Within."*

Law, ignorance of See *ignorance..*

Law, individualizing See *individualizing.*

Law, invoking See *invoking the Law.*

law is, but needs enforcement Laws exist before they are recognized, but must be understood before they can be used.

Law knows no favorites Just as there is neither big nor little in the Law, so there are no important or unimportant people, conditions, or events; It works just as well for one as for another.

Law knows us only as we know ourselves Since the Law of Mind is a reflection from the mental image or cause to physical correspondent or effect, it follows that it only reflects for us, about us, or to us, that which is actually embodied in our thought. In this way every man becomes a law unto himself under the One Great Law.

Law, letter and spirit of the The letter of the Law is the mechanical part of a treatment, our mental statements. The Spirit of the Law is the deep conviction which clothes the statement with life. This is a combination of intellectual and spiritual perception.

Law—letting Law do the work See *letting*.

Law, limitation not inherent in See *limitation is not*.

Law, Love and See *Love and the Law*.

law, mechanical See *Subjective Mind as; thought moves*.

law, mental See *mental law*.

law (mental) as an infinite medium The Law of Mind is without limit in Its ability not only to produce, but also to adapt means to ends; all processes are involved within It.

law (mental) has no intention of its own The Law of Mind, like any other law in nature, is not personal but personalized. (We must not confuse the Law of Mind with the Spirit of God.) Therefore the Law as force, energy, and creative intelligence responds to us only by corresponding with our mental attitudes. In this way we make up Its mind for us, so far as we are concerned.

Law (Mental), One See *One Mental.*

law, mental treatment as See *mental treatment as law.*

Law of Attraction The principle that we attract that to which our thought is attuned.

Law of Averages An impersonal and unconscious acceptance of what the race thought has believed to be true about all people. (See *Averages, Law of.*)

Law of Belief See *Belief, Law of.*

Law of Cause and Effect, of itself, never moves The Law of Mind, like other laws, must be consciously used if it is to produce a definite result. It is always moved upon by the creative word of Spirit. (See *Cause and Effect.*)

Law of Cause and Effect operates automatically Just as the creative soil receives the seed and mechanically and auto matically operates upon it, so the Law of Mind acts upon thought. (See *Cause and Effect.*)

Law of Cause and Effect specialized To create a new sequence in the Law by reflecting a new idea into It, thus causing It to create a form corresponding to the idea reflected. (See *Cause and Effect.*)

Law of Chance Refers to the activity of the collective mind operating in the individual.

Law of Compensation Generally refers to the Emersonian conception of cause and effect. (See *Compensation, Law of.*)

Law of Consciousness One's consciousness consists of one's entire mental life, both conscious and subjective. The sum total of beliefs in this consciousness are, at any moment, the law of one's life.

Law of Correspondents   The subjective world contains an image of everything which is reflected in the objective world. Refers to the theory that the objective universe is projected by an invisible cause which exactly corresponds to it.

Law of Faith   The law Jesus taught when he said: ''According to your faith, be it unto you.'' By this law, which is the ''substance of things hoped for,'' does man bring into his experience the things which he desires.

Law of Giving and Receiving   See *Giving and Receiving.*

Law of Growth   That principle which contains everything necessary to the fulfillment of any idea which has been placed in the creative soil of Mind. As the seed, placed in the ground, must have a definite period of time for the development of the life germ into the perfect plant, so does the Law of Growth require time for the fulfillment of an idea. Man drops an idea into Mind and then remains faithful to it until the Law of Growth delivers to him the manifestation of his idea in form.

Law of Love, under the   The true nature of Reality must be love, unity, and peace; hence a consciousness of Its true nature supersedes all other thoughts of consciousness and heals them. (See *Love and.*)

Law of Mental Equivalents   Whatever is truly embodied in mind finds a corresponding objectification.

Law of Mind confused with Spirit of God   See *superstition.*

Law of Mind in action   Mental treatment rightly understood, given, and believed in, because it operates through the medium of Universal Mind, has within itself the intelligence and the power to project a form which mathematically corresponds to its own awareness. (See *servant.*)

Law of Mind neither good nor bad   We should not confuse the Law of Mind with the Spirit. Mental law, like other laws in nature, is a mechanical force—a doer and not a knower. We could not speak of any laws of nature as being good or evil; we merely speak of the good or evil use of such laws.

Law of Mind, right ideas enforce   See *right ideas enforce.*

Law of Reversal   A belief that either we ourselves, or someone else, can reverse or make negative the action of the mental law toward us.

Law of Self-Approval   Mental and spiritual realization that we are one with the Creative Spirit which always approves of us.

Law of Sequence   The principle that the fruits of any seed planted (be it seed of thought, plant, animal, or man) will be like the seed. From the time of the planting of the seed there will be a sequential train of events, as growth, until the fruits of the seed are manifested.

Law of Spiritual Demonstration   The operation of thought in the Mind Principle is Law.

law of sublimation   See *sublimation, law of.*

Law of Tendency   The principle of Life Itself to create out of Itself life in form and everything that is necessary for its existence. The tendency is toward abundance, good for all. In man's experience, his bodily health and the conditions in his life will take form according to the *tendency of his thought.* If the trend be toward the constructive side of life, there will be a forward and upward movement, along the line of abundance, of good. If the trend be toward negativity or destructive thinking, his experiences and conditions will manifest in a downward tendency, as illness, accidents, lack, etc.

Law of Unity   The Principle of Wholeness in the Universe, which is the basic Law of Life. In it is contained the Law of Continuity.

Law (the) reacts automatically   See *treatment is conscious.*

Law, reversing our use of   See *reversing our use.*

Law (the) says yes when we say yes, no when we way no
Since the Mental Law can only react, it follows that It must react to our thought with mathematical precision, whatever that thought may be. Both yes and no are affirmations of some conviction.

law unto itself, treatment is a   See *treatment is a.*

law unto yourself   Each one individualizes the Creative Principle in a unique way. Every man's word is his law. This law may be consciously used.

law, we do not coerce it   Since the Law of Mind is one of reflection, it is no more necessary to force an image on it that it would be to force an image onto the mirror. The mirror cannot help but reflect the image before it; the Law cannot help but reflect our thought.

Law—we invoke the Law, the Law evolves the form   Like a seed falling into the soil, thought falls into the creative medium of Mind. This is called invoking the Law. That which follows—the act of the Creative Mind producing a form—is called evolution, or the passing of the Law into form.

Law which binds can free   Just as fire will burn us or cook our food, so the Law of Mind will act upon our images of thought, be these images those of freedom or of bondage.

Law works automatically until we change it   Our thought patterns continue to reflect certain conditions until we change such thought patterns. Our use of the Mental Law is an automatic, mechanical, and mathematical reaction to our thought patterns.

laws execute themselves Mental treatment, acting as Law, becomes self-executed; it has within itself everything necessary to propel itself into action.

laws of nature are self-existent and self-sustaining Universal laws were never created; they have always existed. They are co-eternal with Spirit or Reality. Laws and principles always were; we merely apply them.

laws of nature are self-operative All natural laws have the energy within themselves to be self-operative, else they would not be natural laws. In other words, if we had to energize energy, where would we go to get the energy with which to energize it? The proposition becomes self-evident.

left-hand path Symbolic of the destructive use of the creative Power of Mind. Black Magic. Self-will, as opposed to Divine Will, or the Will of God, which can only be of the nature of Good. The path that leads to complete negation, since error destroys itself. (See *black magic*.)

let go and let God To surrender all denial of good, all sense of personal responsibility in treatment, and come spiritually to believe that the Law of Spirit meets the need.

let the dead bury their dead We do not arrive at new truths through repeating ancient mistakes, nor do we gain anything through holding controversy with antiquated beliefs.

"Let there be light" Let the consciousness be illumined with love, peace, and wisdom.

"Let this mind be in you" Permit yourself to believe that all Power, Truth, and Goodness operate through you.

letting the Law do the work It is the business of the practitioner to make his statements in Mind with clarity, conviction, and sincerity, after which he must completely let go of his treatment; it is now in the Law of Cause and Effect.

liberation Freedom. When liberated, one is free from the pairs of opposites.

libido and the Divine Urge Libido may be defined as an emotional craving toward self-expression which is in everything. This psychological term has its correspondent in the Science of Mind in what is called the Divine Urge, or the necessity that the Life Principle shall be expressed.

Life, Fountain of See *Fountain*.

Life, God as See *God as Life*.

Life, inner See *inner Life*.

Life, living See *living the Life*.

Life Principle Has the same meaning as the Law of Spirit.

Life Principle as essence The Divine Spirit; Reality; warm, colorful, personal; God the Spirit; God the Infinite Person; our Father which art in heaven.

Life Principle as Law Law is not a person but a mathematical manifestation. We are surrounded not only by the Universal Spirit but also by the Universal Law. This is the Law of Cause and Effect; unthinking, unfeeling, it knows only to do. Thus it follows our patterns of thought.

lift yourself out of your limitation This means to transcend old thought patterns.

Light See *inner Light*.

likeness of God Man's spiritual nature is God; the difference is not in essence but in degree. (See *image and.*)

limitation and freedom are identical Limitation, being

merely a way of using the Law, is never a thing in itself. A less limited use produces what we call greater freedom. This freedom is never a thing in itself. These are merely two ways of using the same Law.

limitation is not inherent in the Law Like the law of electricity, the Principle of Mind is neither big, little, good, bad, high, low, etc. It is merely something to be used. It must reflect the images of thought imposed upon It.

listening, spiritual See *meditation without.*

living affirmatively Continuously expecting good, happiness, joy, etc.

living the Life Continuously embodying the spirit of Good, of Wholeness, of Harmony, of Love, and of Perfection.

livingness Animate existence, as distinguished from inanimate existence. Conscious existence. Vigorous, active, animated. The power of motion. Since Life Itself is Intelligence, the livingness in any individual expression is estimated according to the degree of intelligence it displays. Spirit is Life, so the livingness in anything is its spiritual essence.

Logos The Divine Creative Word. Probably had a meaning to the ancient Greeks similar to that of Christ to the Christian philosophy.

loneliness healed A recognition that there is one infinite Person in whom all live in a state of cooperative unity heals loneliness.

"Look unto me and be ye saved" In such degree as our thought deals with absolute Unity it automatically provides salvation.

loosing thoughts Refers to the necessity of mentally letting go of one's spiritual treatment after one has given it.

Lord See *"I am the Lord."*

"Lord (the) is in His holy temple" *Temple* refers to the inner sanctuary of the heart: The Lord is both with man and within him.

"Lord (the) is the light of my life" Spiritual thought, faith, and conviction are like a light shining in the darkness.

Lord of hosts A symbol of the Higher Self.

Lord (the) our God is one Lord There is but one creative Causation; one Power; one Presence; one infinite Person. This One is individualized in everything.

"Lord (the) will go before you" Refers to the word of Truth making straight the way.

Lord's Supper The bread and wine representing the flesh and blood, or form and circulation. It represents the solid and the liquid in the universe.

Love The outpouring of Spirit. The givingness of Life. In its lesser sense, the affection one has for another. The Principle of Love is not to be confused with mere sentimentality, although all forms of love are aspects of It. It is the great transforming Power, which brings everything into harmony. It is the unifying Principle, the creative element, the motivating Power of all that is fine and noble in life. In metaphysical treatment it is the healing force. (See *Divine Love; God as Love.*)

Love and the Law The impulsion of the Spirit or the Originating Cause is Love; the operation of Its action is through Law. (See *Law of Love.*)

love as a solvent An inner realization of Love dissolves that which seems opposed to Love.

Love, God as See *God as Love.*

love, science of See *science of love.*

lower and higher self The lower self is that part of our psychological nature which deals only with external facts, which appear to be separated from that which is good, perfect, and holy. The Higher Self means the Christ; the realization of truth; the Spiritual Man; that which is conscious of Its union with goodness, truth, and beauty; that which is always constructive.

lower worlds See *higher*.

lulled to sleep by the race mind The almost hypnotic power of thought patterns which have been believed in throughout the ages.

M

Macrocosm The Universal Mind, Spirit and Law; that within which all things are contained.

"Make known your requests in secret" Accept the desired condition as already accomplished fact; do this inwardly, calmly, peacefully, joyfully, and completely.

making clean the outside of the platter We cannot erase an effect with an effect. The outside is the result of the inside. If inwardly we are whole, then outwardly we shall be made whole.

malinger To feign illness or inability in order to avoid one's duty. All forms of fraud relating to sickness and injury.

malpractice See *mental malpractice*.

Man See *God and Man; ''Who''; wisdom*.

man as a center of God-Consciousness The mind of man is the Divine Mind operating in him. He is a center of God in God. (See *God is our*.)

man as a reflection of God Refers to the belief that man reflects perfection as an image is reflected in a mirror. Refers to the generic or universal man, which the Bible calls Christ, as a complete and perfect manifestation of the parent Mind which we call God, reflecting, imaging, or manifesting Its entire perfection. Each individual is called a member of this Body; thus Jesus said, "I am the Vine, ye are the branches." (See *Perfection.*)

man as mind instead of idea The Mind of God is also the mind of man. An absolute union of man with God. One Being and One Mind.

man as the realization of God Man is the Self-Knowingness of God; the Consciousness of God in execution; the Action of God moving into fulfillment; the Thought of God seeking self-expression.

man as the shadow of a rock Refers to our spiritual nature as a hiding place from harm.

man, difference between God and See *difference.*

man is God's identity The universal and cosmic Self is invisible. This invisible Presence is identified in each person as It is individualized through him. That which is manifest alone gives absolute proof of the invisible.

man is universal subjectivity Just as there is One common Mind spiritually, which is God, so there is One common Subjective Law of Mind. Man is omnipresent both spiritually and subjectively.

man, nature waits on See *nature waits.*

man, only one Since man is the consciousness of God, and since God's consciousness is one consciousness, there is but One Man. This Man is universal. This is what the Bible calls the Christ.

man reveals God The consciousness of man is the only thing we know of that has any knowledge of God, merely because the consciousness of man is the only thing man knows of, or about, that has any consciousness of anything. Thus man alone reveals God.

man, Spirit of See *"Spirit (the) of man."*

"man's foes (a) shall be they of his own household" Our foes are our thoughts.

man's real entity Consists of the sum total of his understanding.

manna from heaven The outpouring of Spirit.

manvantara A world period, an age.

martyr One who sacrifices life, position, etc, for a principle or to sustain a cause.

mastery That state of being where one rules, or governs, one's own thoughts and actions.

material plane Objectivity; world of form; manifestation; result.

materialization Refers to the psychic forming of parts or the whole of a human body by supernormal means.

matter, mind over See *mind over.*

matter seen as Mind Matter, or the physical world, is not one thing while Mind is another; they are identical. The physical universe is Mind in form. (See *Mind is.*)

matter, spiritualizing See *spiritualizing; we neither.*

matter, unreality of This does not deny the physical body or other physical objects; it merely affirms that all form is the manifestation of the energy of Mind. Mind is Substance and projects form.

maya Refers to the possibility of the subconscious mind

presenting us with illusion. Might refer to psychic confusion or to the world psyche.

meditation Mentally dwelling upon an idea in order that one consciously may become aware of its meaning.

meditation, our universe as our See *our universe.*

meditation, Universe as God's See *Universe as the.*

meditation with words Silent treatment consciously thought.

meditation without words Consciously centering the thought on some idea without using any mental form of treatment. Spiritual listening. Definite spiritual acceptance without argument or mental controversy.

"members in one body . . . and members one of another" A symbolic description of the unity of all life.

memory, stream of Individually: the imprint of experience, mental or objective, within the compass of one's immediate individualized mind. Collectively: the sum total of all human experiences; the Akashic records. The stream of memory may be both individual and racial, or worldwide. This corresponds to the individual unconscious and the collective unconscious of Jungian psychology.

mental adjustment Adjusting one's emotional and intellectual thought patterns to circumstances, situations, or conditions as they must be met in the world of objective reality.

mental analysis for spiritual realization Repudiating the thought that anything is wrong in the universe, or that there is some place where something is wrong; or that there is a sequence of time or cause and effect which either created, sustains, or brings about anything wrong; or that there is any material existence or *any* existence separated from Spirit in which anything wrong could be formed; or that there is any Law or medium for such wrong formation. Analysis follows with a realization that Spirit, being ever present, constitutes the only place there is. Spirit, being the only time, is the Eternal Now. The substance of everything is pure Spirit, the Law of everything is pure Good. The word which declares this is the Presence, the Power, and Activity of this Good asserting Itself.

mental atmosphere   The subjective atmosphere which surrounds all persons and all things.

mental attitude   The trend of one's thought, which may be positive or negative, constructive or destructive. This attitude is the determining factor of the experiences of life, as well as the kind of environment.

mental diagnosis   Uncovering mental causes. Judging the operation of invisible mental causes through observing their objective effects.

mental equivalent   The conscious subjective image of thought which is the cause of the external or corresponding condition.

mental equivalent for right action   The consciousness of success in everything one undertakes.

mental equivalent representing the bloodstream   The idea of Life flowing, purifying, vivifying, energizing.

Mental Equivalents, Law of   See *Law of Mental Equivalents.*

mental healing is clear thinking followed by definite statement   The clear thinking affirms the Allness of God, Good, Light, Truth, etc. The definite statements affirm this Allness while denying any reality to Its opposite.

mental image   The ability of the imagination to form mental pictures, a phase of the creative process. Subjective likeness; mental equivalent; mental correspondent; etc.

mental influence   Any suggestion which we take on from the thought of others or from the race thought.

mental law follows one pattern as quickly as another   Just as the creative soil produces one plant as quickly as another, so the Law of Mind follows the pattern of thought given It.

mental law is a mathematical sequence of cause and effect   It starts with Absolute Intelligence; next, the movement of Intelligence, which is the Word; then the operation of the Law, which obeys the Word; next, the manifestation of the Word through Law. The only spontaneous element in this entire sequence is the speaking of the word; everything that follows is mechanical. (See *Cause and Effect, sequence; sequence of causation.*)

mental law never initiates, it always reacts   Only conscious intelligence can initiate; subconscious intelligence has no choice other than to accept.

mental law, no big and no little in   Since all created things are but forms in mind and never things in themselves, the reflection of what we call big is neither more nor less than the reflection of what we call small. The only thing within us which decides is our mental equivalent.

Mental Law, One   See *One Mental.*

mental malpractice   Refers to the mistaken idea that people can use the Principle of Good to produce evil.

mental medium   Has reference to the universal subjectivity, which is the medium for thought.

mental plane   Realm of thought; mind; consciousness.

mental spiritual treatment   Spiritualizing the thought in mental treatment. (See *mental treatment; spiritual treatment; treat; treating; treatment.*)

mental therapeutics Mind healing.

mental treatment as an act, art, and science It is an act, being the conscious activity of thought; it is an art in that there must be feeling, appreciation, and realization; it is a science, in that it deals with a mathematical law of cause and effect.

mental treatment as law The ideas used in mental treatment as an intelligent but mathematical law. A statement of Truth acting as law; therefore spiritual mind treatment is the Law of Mind in action.

mental treatment cannot heal another unless it first heals yourself Since in spiritual treatment one's word uses a power which is loosed through that word and at the level of that word's embodiment, it follows that in this practice one really clears up one's own thought of what appears to be wrong with others, for "if the blind lead the blind, shall they both not fall into the ditch?"

mental treatment, correcting mistakes in Consciously recognizing the wrong belief or pattern of thought, and, by reversing it, consciously recognizing the opposite, which is Truth.

mental treatment, getting out of our own way in Just as a gardener would get out of the way in letting the seed grow, so we must give our treatment, feeling that there is a Law which will execute it.

mental treatment—in treating one speaks not to his patient but about him Spiritual treatment is neither mental suggestion nor coercion; it is something the practitioner realizes within himself about his patient or about the condition which he seeks to help.

mental treatment is actively conscious of good Spiritual mind treatment consists of more than passively recogniz-

ing God as the only power; it is active in declaring that
this Power is present wherever the need appears to be.

mental treatment, mathematics of The consciousness or
inner awareness must find a corresponding outlet which
will be an exact and mathematical reproduction of the
image of thought which projects it.

mental treatment not a game of chance Mental treatment
demonstrates a mathematical principle; there is no chance
in it. The demonstration is certain to take place at the
level of our own comprehension. Hence, all time in treatment is devoted to the purpose of creating such inward
comprehension; its manifestation will be automatic.

**mental treatment which is conscious consciousness auto-
matically reflects new conditions** *Consciousness* means
one's inner perception of life; one's interior awareness.
When consciousness is reorganized in conformity with
Truth, it automatically reflects a new impulse to the physical body and creates a new situation in objective affairs.
Since consciousness is the real cause of form, and since
form is merely a reflection of consciousness, it follows that
wherever consciousness is changed, form automatically
must change to comply with the new image of thought.
(See *conditions; causes and conditions.*)

mental work always definite A mental treatment is neither
day-dreaming, wistful wishing, nor hallucination; it consists either of denying that which ought not to be and
affirming that which ought to be, or of silent recognition
of perfection. It is always conscious, active, and dynamic.

mesmerized by pain When the experience of pain becomes
so severe that it is seemingly impossible mentally to turn
to a state of peace, treat to annihilate fear; mentally work
until the entire consciousness is lifted from fear into faith.

Messiah A great spiritual teacher and leader. A perfect manifestation of life, as man. The Divine Son of God, having all power and all wisdom. One who comes to teach and liberate humanity. Spiritual thought force is the Messiah. Refers to the higher self in every man.

metaphysical healing versus faith cure Metaphysical practice consists of definite and conscious use of the Law of Mind within the thought of the one using it. Faith cure refers to the act of one individual praying that God will do something to another individual. In the one instance the practitioner understands what he is doing, in the other he has faith that some power will respond to his prayer.

metaphysics That which is beyond the known laws of physics. Refers to what are considered unknown but intelligent forces latent in the human mind. (See *objective metaphysics; subjective metaphysics.*)

metaphysics applied Viewing the universe as a mental spiritual system, governed by laws of thought. Man, being part of this system, discovers the same laws inherent within his own being and may apply them for definite purposes.

microcosm An individualized center within the Macrocosm, containing within itself the essence of Reality.

mighty-armed All-powerful, having those qualities of courage, strength, wisdom, divine tranquillity, etc., which give one a sense of mastery.

Mind Mind in a conscious state has the same meaning as Spirit. Mind as law means the subjective reaction of thought, or the Law of Mind in action. (See *Law of Mind in action; Law of Mind neither good nor bad; One Body.*)

Mind, all-inclusive Cause, medium, and effect; law, consciousness, power; action and reaction—all are included in Mind.

mind as a law of elimination   A spiritual consciousness of perfect circulation and perfect assimilation is a law of elimination to physical congestions, wrong conditions, etc.

Mind as a mirror   Subjective Creative Mind has no choice other than to receive the images of our thought and reflect them back to us as conditions. (See *mirror.*)

Mind as a servant of the Spirit   Means that the creative Law of Cause and Effect obeys, and is the servant of, the directive word.

Mind can only operate upon ideas   Since the Mind Principle is at the root of everything, and since the only activity of Mind is idea, then the only movement of Mind is upon idea. It also follows that wherever there is idea, the Creative Principle must operate upon it.

mind cannot accept what it rejects   We cannot have what we will not take, and since the taking is mental, we can only have what we accept.

Mind, Divine   See *Divine Mind.*

mind, individual   Spirit, God, the Absolute, acting in and through man.

Mind is not one thing and the physical universe another   Philosophic conception of Spinoza that mind and matter are identical. Since there is nothing but Mind, Reality, or Spirit, and what It does, and since what It does is the projection of Itself within Itself and upon Itself, then all manifestation is Mind in form. Since form is bound to the principle which projects it, by the law of reflection, form or reflection cannot be divorced from the consciousness which projects it.

mind, man as   See *man as mind.*

Mind, nothing but   See *nothing but.*

Mind, One for all people   See *One Mind.*

Mind, only One   See *only One Mind.*

mind over matter   Refers to the misconception that a spiritual treatment operates upon a material substance.

Mind Power   Mind Power exists around us and within us like the ethers. Thought acts upon this Power as Law.

Mind receives our petition and answers our prayer   Since Mind is omnipresent and ever-receptive, It cannot refuse to listen, nor can It refuse to operate upon our thought.

mind, renewing the   See *renewing.*

Mind, Self-Knowing   See *Self-Knowing Mind.*

Mind, Subjective   See *Subjective Mind.*

mind, subliminal   See *subliminal mind.*

mind surgery   A conscious mental act of so completely recognizing the Principle of Perfection that the false condition is dissolved. A definite belief that this is taking place as a result of a treatment consciously given.

mind (the) that was in Christ Jesus   The universal sense of goodness and unity upon which Jesus based his thinking.

Mind the only actor   The inner movement of the Infinite Mind produces all creation; all action in creation is Mind taking form; all Law is Mind in action.

mind, thinking center in   See *thinking.*

mind, transformed by the renewal of   As habitual thought patterns are changed, an outward transformation takes place which exactly corresponds with the inner spiritual awareness. (See *transformed.*)

Mind, Universal   See *Universal Mind.*

mind, unwavering   See *unwavering.*

mind's silent partner   Refers to the Law of Cause and Effect, which obeys the conscious use of it.

miracle In its narrowest meaning, supernaturalism; an interference, by the Divine, of the laws of the universe; special providence. In its broader sense, *miracle* means that which is not supernatural but supernormal and is above and beyond the average experience and viewpoint. In the sense in which we use it, the word *miracle* means a wonderful result of the creative power of thought.

mirror of mind Subjective life acts like a mirror reflecting the forms of thought that are given to it. Mind acts like a mirror, reflecting the images of our thoughts back to us exactly as we think them.

mistake See *practitioner must rise above.*

monad of life The symbol of Spirit differentiated in human souls.

monogenesis The development of all life from One Originating Source by the action of Spirit upon Itself.

mortal and immortal mind Since there is but One Mind, which is God, all Mind is immortal. By the mortal, carnal, or human mind is meant any misstatement about, or misunderstanding of, Reality. Mortal mind refers to the belief that there is a mind separate from God; that man is in some way disconnected from the Universal. A suppositional opposite to good.

Most High One The One Divine Spirit unfolding at the center of man's consciousness. This One Spirit is the same in every person.

Mother See *Divine Mother.*

mountain or mount Consciousness functioning on the plane of spiritual realization.

mountaintop The highest form of consciousness.

movement of consciousness upon itself Refers to the self-contemplation of Spirit, or the action of Life upon Itself, which is the initial movement of creation. (See *consciousness—movement.*)

movement of Spirit is an interior movement   There is nothing that Spirit can move upon except Itself, and nowhere It can move other than within Itself; therefore all movement is inward, upon Itself.

movement of thought   Refers to any act of consciousness within the self.

multiplicity in unity   All things come from one fundamental Unity. (See *One Unit; Oneness can.*)

music of the spheres   The rhythmic harmony that flows through everything.

my consciousness is God   In such degree as our consciousness operates at all, it must operate in and upon the Creative Principle. In this sense it is God.

"My Father worketh hitherto, and I work"   Refers to the evolutionary process which arbitrarily compels man to evolve to the point of self-determination, freedom, volition; from this point man's further evolution results from his conscious cooperation with the Creative Principle.

"My Lord and My God"   The Presence within me which is complete, perfect, and whole. (See *God in me.*)

"My yoke is easy and my burden is light"   The Spirit does not enter into conflict or labor. The process of creation is painless, peaceful, and without effort.

mystical marriage   Conscious union of the individual "I" with the universal "I Am." The conscious at-one-ment with the Source of Being, God. A consciousness of the unity of all life. The joining of the Great Self, the God-in-man, with the little self, or the limited human consciousness.

mysticism The inward awareness of the divine Presence in all things. Not to be confused with mystery, nor with psychism. A mystic is one who intuitionally senses Reality.

N

Name, in His In compliance with the nature of Reality.

Nature See *Divine Nature*.

nature as the great nothing Term used by Neo-Platonists to express the idea that the visible universe is not a thing in itself; it means that nature is no-thing in itself—it is an effect of that which projects it.

Nature of God forever unfolding Since Reality is infinite in all of Its aspects and since we are forever discovering new truths, nature of necessity ever unfolds itself to us through our experience.

nature unaided fails This saying, ascribed to Hermes, means that the laws of nature must be consciously used before they will do definite things for us. This is just as true of the laws of mind as it is of the laws of electricity. God can do for us only what He can do through us. We should cooperate with and specialize the laws of nature.

nature waits on man Ancient saying in reference to the self-evident truth that natural laws, which also include spiritual laws, may be consciously used only after they are discovered and understood.

negation, do not dwell on Think of negation only as something which has no law to support it; deny its existence in Reality and turn at once to its opposite, which is the Truth.

negation, impersonalizing See *impersonalizing negation*.

negative suggestions See *collective negative.*

negative thinking Thinking with reference to opposites. (See *hypnotic.*)

negatives, reversing See *reversing our negatives.*

"Neither do I condemn thee" The Spirit never condemns, but Its judgment is always correct, since the Law of Cause and Effect is immutable.

nerves as a manifestation of intelligence In spiritual treatment one works to know that the entire nervous system is a manifestation of Infinite Intelligence, in which there is no irritation, agitation, or inflammation.

neutralize fear with faith Definite treatment declaring for the presence of Goodness, Peace, Joy, etc., until the negative state of fear disappears from the mind.

neutralize—it is possible for one to neutralize his own effort If certain modes of thinking produce certain results, then opposite modes of thought will produce opposite results. However, we should always remember that true thought overcomes all unlike itself, as light dissipates darkness.

neutralizing thought Conscious act of mentally erasing negative thought impulses.

never too late In mental treatment, no matter what the previous experience may have been, a new creation is about to take place in a timeless universe.

New Thought A system of thought which affirms the unity of God with man, the perfection of all life, and the immortality and eternality of the individual soul forever expanding.

New Thought applied The conscious use of the laws of thought for the purpose of producing betterment in one's life or in the lives of others.

New Thought Movement Groups, societies, religious and spiritual organizations built upon the New Thought philosophy, leaving room for ample independent individualism. The principles governing the New Thought Movement are universal but individually and independently applied.

Nirvana In its broadest sense, a state of bliss.

no life separated from God Since there is but One Mind, or final Causation, each must not only partake of Its nature, but must actually be Its nature in manifestation.

"No man hath ascended up to heaven but he that came down from heaven, even the Son of man which is in heaven" It would be impossible to go to Heaven unless our nature originated in Heaven, and since all Reality is One, and ever present, we are already in Heaven, could we but comprehend Its harmony.

no one to convince but yourself In mental treatment one's entire endeavor is to straighten out one's own thought about the person or the condition one is working for.

no reason for Truth There never was a time when Truth began to be true. God did not make Truth, since God is Truth, therefore the Truth is that which Is.

"No weapon that is formed against Thee shall prosper" When consciousness functions from the standpoint of spiritual awareness, nothing can destroy its effect.

"None is good save one, that is God" There is only One Creative Cause; nothing flows from It but goodness.

"Not by power nor by might but by my Spirit" All power is spiritual; all law is Mind in action.

not individual but individualized *Individual* would imply separation and disunion; *individualized* means many points of consciousness in One Mind.

"Not that which goeth into the mouth defileth a man, but that which cometh out of the mouth" It is not the suggestion which our environment reflects to us, but our reaction to it which does the damage.

nothing but what Mind is and what It does The One Infinite Mind, being all Cause, must also be all effect. Hence what we call our mind is this Mind in us. This Mind, through our own awareness, is presenting us either with subjective hallucination and objective confusion or with subjective union and objective peace, according to the way we use this Mind. Our world, both mental and physical, is either an outpouring of some adequate concept of the union of all life, or else it is an outpicturing of a misconception of such unity. (See *there is nothing but.*)

Noumenon The Spirit, or innermost essence; the root of anything; that which makes it an individual thing.

nucleus In physical science, a core, or kernel. A center around which matter gathers. In the psychic life a nucleus is created through thought. It may be thought of fear or faith; constructive or destructive; but whatever it is, it will attract like matter to it. It does this if undisturbed, or not neutralized, until an external form, corresponding to the nucleus, comes into manifestation on the form side of life. It is an illustration of the ''Law of Correspondences.'' According to the idea held in mind, which creates the nucleus, the corresponding manifestation appears on the material plane.

O

obedience to the Divine Law Conscious union and cooperation with the Divine Nature that is Goodness, Truth, Beauty, etc.

objective   Expression outwardly, or in a positive manner, as opposed to subjective, or introversion. Outward form.

objective metaphysics   Raps, levitation, apparitions, etc.

objective plane   The outer world of expression and experience.

objective world   The world of conditions.

objective world as cinema pictures   A term used by certain groups to express the idea that the entire visible universe is a moving picture of subjective thoughts which project it.

oblation   In church ritual the act of offering to God the Eucharistic elements (bread and wine), in token of devotion and sacrifice. In metaphysics oblation means to sacrifice the self to the Self—that is, the human frailties of anger, dishonesty, criticism, dislike, etc., are laid on the altar of Divine Love as a sacrifice to the God-Self, that the human self may be merged completely with the Divine.

obligation (personal) in treatment   See *personal responsibility.*

obstetrics, spiritual   Conscious realization that physical birth is the self-recognition of Spirit breathing Itself into form.

octave   The term is founded on the number eight, as in the musical scale. The eighth note is a repetition of the first, but in a higher sequence, or octave. Thus the end of one series of musical sounds is the beginning of another. The term is used in spiritual teaching, in that Life is a continual unfoldment, that which develops being dependent upon that which has gone before.

"of the earth, earthy"   Refers to any state of consciousness based upon a merely material conception.

ointment   Symbolizes Divine Love or the Divine Nature.

old age Arises from the belief that there is a beginning and an end of Reality. As a matter of fact, the experiences of tomorrow are not yet born, hence every day marks a perennial dawn, an everlasting here and an eternal now.

Om (Aum) The most holy word of the Vedas. A symbolic word meaning the Supreme Being, the Divine, or Deity. The Logos. Sound. The Word. Bliss Absolute. Signifies that "which has been, that which is, and that which is to be."

omega The last letter of the Greek alphabet. Symbolizes the end.

Omnipotence—Omnipresence—Omniscience Spirit is All Power, All Presence, and All Wisdom.

Omnipotence within me The Power of the Absolute at the center of my own being.

omnipotent in power, omniscient in wisdom, omnipresent in being Since the Infinite is an indivisible Unity, Its entire nature is always at the point of our attention.

Omnipresence See *God's ideas; man is universal; Omnipotence.*

Omnipresence within me The Presence of God, Spirit, Reality, at the center of my own being. "The Highest God and the innermost God is One God."

omnipresent See *omnipotent.*

Omniscience See *Omnipotence.*

Omniscience in me The All-Knowing Mind at the center of my own being.

omniscient See *omnipotent.*

Once-Born The First Birth is the awakening of the consciousness to its natural environment with a sense of isolation and separateness; anything that designates purely physical or material; anything that designates merely mental, lacking the consciousness of eternal Goodness or Divine Union.

One Body, One Spirit, One Mind   Spiritually we are one with God as Absolute Intelligence. Mentally there is one Law of Mind which we all use, and physically all manifest forms are but different rates of vibration of one fundamental stuff. (See *only One Body; only One Mind.*)

One Mental Law   Since there is but One Mind, there is but one Law of Mind. We each individualize this Law, thus each becomes a law unto himself in the One Law.

One Mind for all people   There is but One Mind which each one individualizes.

one place, one time, one Substance, one Spirit, and one Law   This realization should be carefully considered in every treatment in order to bring the effect of the treatment into the immediate experience.

One Presence   There is but One Universe, One Creative Spirit, One Life Principle, in, around, and through everything. This One is also the Presence within man—the True Self.

One Unit, many manifestations   Just as mathematics has one final unit with countless expressions, so there is but One Mind Principle in the universe with innumerable expressions.

Oneness can produce multiplicity but not duality   Duality supposes opposing fundamental principles. One principle, however, can produce innumerable forms, personalities, etc., without in any way denying its unity.

oneness with Spirit makes our thought creative   Our thought is not creative because we either will or wish it to be so; rather it is creative because this is its nature.

Only-Begotten Son A son begotten of the Only Father. (See *Beloved Son; Father and.*)

only One Body The entire manifest universe is the body of God; as there is One Mind, there is One Body; this Body is perfect.

only One Mind The mind which we use in giving treatment, or in thinking at any time, is the Mind of God in us.

only those who recognize spiritual power can have conscious use of it Even though all people already are endowed with spiritual power, one must consciously believe in and use it if one hopes to get definite results.

ontology The science of being, or reality. The branch of metaphysics that investigates nature; essential properties and relation of being as such. The doctrine of the universal and necessary characteristics of all existence.

opposites, the pairs of The principle of duality, or two opposing forces, as light and darkness, heat and cold, male and female, positive and negative, etc. These principles are found in most ancient religions, as well as in the Christian. However, the term does not necessarily mean conflict, but rather balancing forces. They are really the two ends of a pole. On the physical plane, often referred to as "the shadow world," or the "world of illusion," man swings between these pairs of opposites—joy and despair, sickness and health, etc. As he becomes illumined, and rises in his thought to the plane of Reality, at the apex of the triangle, as it is symbolized, he sees the pairs of opposites in their true light as one—the two ends of the base of the triangle.

"Or ever the silver cord be loosed" Refers to a complete psychic severance from the physical body. When the silver, or psychic cord is loosed, then there is complete separation; physical disintegration sets in because the spirit is freed from the body.

organs and functions as spiritual ideas All organs and functions of the body are ideas and manifestations of spiritual perfection. There is no organ or function separate from the idea.

origin of evil Evil has no origin, for if it did, the universe would be divided against itself, and the discovery of truth would produce bondage. There never was a time when two and two made five.

original sin The state of ignorance which exists in mind before it discovers its true relationship to the universe.

Originating Spirit The Eternal Reality back of all forms of Life. That which has brought everything that exists into being. The Absolute.

"Our bloated nothingness" Any and all mental concepts which confuse effects with causes.

our Redeemer Right ideas definitely stated and completely believed in. (See *Redeemer*.)

our salvation Definite, conscious, and active knowledge that right ideas heal, change conditions, etc. (See *salvation*.)

our universe as our meditation The reproduction of the cosmos in the individual life.

our within lies open to the Infinite Since there is but One Mind which we use, it follows that there is a place within each one of us which merges with the Infinite. The Over-Soul, Over-Self, or Christ Principle within us is a direct and unique impartation of the Universal Spirit through us. There is a place within us which knows the answer to every problem, knows how to meet every situation; it is boundless, free, and perfect.

outlining in treatment Not to be confused with choice. Outlining means definitely determining just how a demonstration shall be made. We do not outline, but we do choose.

outward correspondent of inner realization   Conditions are like images reflected in a mirror; mind is the mirror, thought is the image, condition is the reflection.

over all, in all, and through all   The one creative Principle permeating everything as Mind, as Substance, and as form.

overcoming evil with good   Bringing the light of truth to bear upon the belief in, or the experience of, evil.

Over-Self   The Spirit of God, which is also individualized as the spirit of man.

Over-Soul   Refers to the Universal Mind, or the Universal Spirit.

P

pain, treatment for   A realization of its opposite, which is peace, calmness, joy, and perfect circulation.

pairs of opposites   A belief in good and evil; truth and error; heaven and hell; love and hate; etc. (See *opposites*.)

parable   A symbolic presentation illustrating the relationship between the visible and the invisible; between the laws of nature and the laws of Spirit.

parable of the sower   Represents ideas which fall into the parent or productive mental soil.

parallel between physical and spiritual laws   Emersonian concept that spiritual, physical, and mental laws are identical; that the spiritual universe is reproduced by an objective one and that we may interpret the spiritual by rightly understanding the physical.

particular, the As the Universal Spirit of Life manifests on the physical plane, It manifests in different modes of existence as the Particular. It can only manifest in form *as* form, the Particular.

Passover, symbol of Passage from the lower to the higher nature; from mental to spiritual planes.

past, not bound by the Since the Creative Principle is forever free from any condition, It is never bound by anything that has happened. However, our *belief* that what happened yesterday must create our experience today does bind us. We must become free from this belief.

path The Journey of Life that leads through experience to union with the Source of Being.

patient One suffering physically, mentally, emotionally; one limited in personal relationships to life; one lacking friendship, opportunity for self-expression; one who is impoverished. Many metaphysical teachers and practitioners refer to such a one as a student rather than as a patient. *Patient* suggests negation while *student* suggests one who needs to become instructed, or who needs to be led, into the affirmative side of life.

patterns of thought Subjective thought atmospheres pertaining to any condition, situation, etc.; habitual and largely unconscious mental attitudes tending to perpetuate themselves.

peace Perfect harmony, well-being. Peace is not an absence of activity, but a very vital, vibrant quality of joyous serenity, where everything is in harmonious relationship.

peace is at the center of everything The eternal equilibrium of the universe is never even temporarily disturbed; there is a place within us which is this equilibrium.

Pearl of great price Symbolizes the Kingdom of Heaven enfolded within the Higher Self.

Perfect as the heavenly Father is perfect The indwelling Spirit within us is God. As consciousness becomes aware of this, all conditions and situations, including the physical body, are lifted up, regenerated, born again.

perfect body A spiritual understanding does not mean a denial of the physical body, but an affirmation that it is a body of spiritual ideas forever perfect, forever harmonious, and forever one with the Eternal Principle of its being, which is God.

perfect universe Since Perfect Cause must produce perfect effect, and since Causation must be perfect in order not to be self-destructive, it follows that there is a perfect universe, even though we may imperfectly perceive it.

perfection See *Spirit ordains*.

Perfection of God is the perfection of man *God* means the Creative Principle of which man is a projection, an emanation, a reflection, an impartation, or an incarnation, whichever expression one desires to use. The effect must be like its Cause. Since there is but One Ultimate Mind which we use and One Ultimate Spirit in which we live, and since this Reality is perfect and is our life, then this perfection is our perfection whether we are conscious of the fact or not.

persistence in prayer To continue treating, praying, meditating, until consciousness is changed, from which change there inevitably follows a demonstration.

Person See *Infinite Person*.

personal choice is Divine Freedom Without choice there would be no spontaneous volition, and without the possibility of more than one experience to choose, there would be no choice; hence Divine Freedom implies the possibility not of real limitation, but of experiencing apparent limitation until, through experience, consciousness increases.

personal responsibility and obligation in treatment It is our obligation to give a treatment if we have contracted to do so; the responsibility of its fulfillment is in the Law of Cause and Effect. (See *healing, no responsibility*.)

personality The objective manifestation of individuality. The use made of individuality. Personality may become acquired or remolded; individuality is always a unique manifestation of the Infinite and cannot be changed. Sum total of all experiences as they manifest in our actions. Popularly, the physical and mental qualities of the individual as they impress others. Metaphysically, personality is the use we make of individuality.

personality is neither evil nor an illusion We do not deny personality, we merely affirm its union with the Infinite. Man is a center of God consciousness in Infinite Mind. He is the personality of God.

personalizing belief in evil The sum total of human thought about evil, devil, Satan, etc., creates an image of belief which operates through all people and which has even apparently been seen by certain persons while in a psychic state. For example, Martin Luther was supposed to have actually seen the devil, and yet there is no real devil. Therefore he must have mentally seen a personification of a belief in evil.

personalness of God The Spirit is personal to each one of us, since It is personified through us.

phantoms of the dead   Subjectively seeing people who have passed on; apparitions of those who have left this world.

phantoms of the living   Subjectively seeing people who are alive; the apparitions of living persons.

philosophic dualism   Any belief in more than one ultimate power, such as good and evil; any belief that there is a material universe separated from a spiritual universe, etc. (See *duality.*)

philosophy   Any man's opinion about anything.

physical body is never denied   In spiritual mind healing we do not deny the physical body; we affirm it to be a body of spiritual ideas.

physical brain   Represents the capacity of the mind to think, know, understand, etc.

physical organs as ideas of mind rather than forms of matter   We do not deny arms, legs, lungs, etc.; we affirm that they are perfect ideas of mind reflecting the Divine.

physical science deals only with the physical   Physical science, as such, ignores the mental and spiritual, hence it often denies the Reality of that Intelligence which makes it possible for the physicist to build, equip, or run a laboratory.

"Physician heal thyself"   Before we can heal others, we must first heal ourselves.

physician to the soul   One who heals the mind.

play of Life upon Itself   All creation is a result of the Creative Spirit operating upon Itself and fulfilling Its desires ouf of the Law of Its own being.

pleasing in the sight of God   Cannot refer to a God who is either pleased or displeased as human beings are, but refers to that which cooperates with the Divine Reality— thus, partaking of its nature, partaking too of Its power.

Polarity, Law of The necessity that every definite idea held in mind shall produce an exact correspondent; the Law responds by corresponding. The result of a mental treatment is a reflected condition which exactly corresponds with the image of thought held before the mirror of mind.

positive Opposite to negative. That which is definite, affirmative, constructive, certain, direct, outgoing.

positive thinking Thinking without reference to opposites.

poverty Belief in lack, or lack of the manifestation of abundance. (See *fasting from poverty*.)

poverty thought An impoverished thought; a denial of good; a limited sense of life. (See *fasting from poverty*.)

power—belief is not the power but the avenue through which it flows Just as in electricity the generator, the dynamo, and the distributor are not the electrical power, but the mechanical instruments through which it flows for specific uses, so faith and belief are mechanical, mental avenues through which a power, already existing, flows into definite use.

Power is not created by us—we use It We never create life nor the forces of nature. Because we live and because these forces exist, we use them. They are all self-executing. The Law of Mind is a natural law.

Power is not injected into mind We take power out of Mind, we do not put it in. The Principle of Power exists and we use It. This is true of every law of nature. All the laws of nature are self-executing. This is also true of Mind, which makes things out of Itself by Itself becoming the thing It makes. Man is not a creator; he is a user of that which already exists. In a certain sense, he breaks it down into different combinations.

Power is; we use It The creative energy of Mind already exists; we merely use it in definite ways. (See *invoking*.)

Power, Mind See *Mind Power*.

power of a mental treatment The spiritual conviction which is arrived at.

power of right ideas See *right ideas, power of*.

power, spiritual—released through thinking See *spiritual power*.

power, tuning into See *tuning into power*.

power (the) we seek we already possess Power *is;* we use it. It already exists at the center of our being. We should learn to use It consciously and constructively.

powers—two ultimate powers impossible See *two*.

practical Christianity Applying the principles which Jesus taught to everyday problems.

practice—in practice you convince yourself A spiritual mind treatment takes place entirely in the thought of the one giving it. The practitioner never seeks to convince anyone but himself no matter whom he is treating or for what purpose.

practice is not something we do but something we know The application of spiritual mind practice rests entirely on the theory that spiritual truth known is demonstrated. There is nothing we can do to the Creative Principle other than to recognize It as operating.

practice, teaching without See *teaching*.

practicing spiritual science The process of realizing and affirming Truth.

practicing the Presence of God A conscious and continuous attempt to feel the Divine Presence in and through everything. Consciously sustaining an interior awareness of God.

practicing the Truth A conscious application of the spiritual Principle to the alleviation of human needs.

practitioner See *separate; spiritual healer; suggestion; treat; treating; treatment; words.*

practitioner clothes his patient with love All spiritual practice must cast out fear and recognize the presence of love, peace, and joy.

practitioner heals himself of any belief in the necessity of the condition from which his patient suffers Since all mental practice is in the medium of the One Mind, and since we neither hold thought, send out thoughts, nor seek to concentrate anything, it is self-evident that all a practitioner could do would be to straighten up his own thought about his patient.

practitioner is the first one to be healed Since all mental practice is something the practitioner does to himself, it follows that he must heal himself of any belief in the necessity of the wrong he wishes to heal in another.

practitioner must have confidence Words without sincere conviction, deep meaning, and complete acceptance in the mind of the practitioner cannot be effective.

practitioner must rise above both mistake and its consequence Since mistake, which is the sin or the wrongdoing, is an error in judgment, and since the consequence is the result of this error, and since it is the practitioner's business to heal both the mistake in judgment and its consequence, it follows that the practitioner must rise in consciousness to the realization where there is neither mistake nor consequence.

practitioner must rise above both wrong physical reactions and wrong mental reactions To the practitioner both the mental state which produces a wrong condition and the wrong condition produced are one and the same thing, since one is the cause of the other. The practitioner must not believe in the spiritual reality of either.

practitioner never condemns patients It is the office of a practitioner to correct mistakes, never to condemn them. He cannot do good work if he sits in judgment on anyone. This is also recognized to be true in the science of psychology.

practitioner or healer A practitioner is one who consciously practices spiritual awareness for himself and others. The Life Principle Itself is the Healer.

practitioner, scientific attitude for See *scientific attitude.*

practitioner, spiritual: never enters into a psychic state Spiritual practice is always consciously directed. A treatment is always conscious, self-assertive, and directive.

praise and thanksgiving A joyful recognition of the Divine Presence combined with a sense of gratitude. A joyous and enthusiastic acceptance.

pray with thanksgiving To be so certain that the demonstration is made, or the prayer answered, that we actually acknowledge it by giving thanks. Joyful acceptance; enthusiastic belief.

pray without ceasing Never stop thinking affirmatively.

prayer Silent contemplation of the Divine Presence ever stimulating the thought, and the universal Law of Mind ever acting. The act of becoming still and knowing that God, the Creative Wisdom and Power, is moving in, upon, and through our affairs. (See *scientific prayer;* *"This kind";* *"When thou."*)

prayer as a unifying process True prayer elevates the consciousness to a recognition of the unity of all life. It is neither petition, supplication, nor despair; rather it is recognition, unification, and communion.

prayer as communion and prayer as petition For prayer as communion, see immediately above. Prayer as petition means adding to communion the conscious recognition that some definite need is met or some specific good is attained.

prayer, highest form of Seeking conscious union with God.

prayer is its own answer The answer to prayer, in accord with cause and effect, is made possible through the belief, acceptance, faith, expectancy of the one praying.

prayer, Mind answers See *Mind receives.*

prayer of faith Quiet contemplation of the Allness of Spirit, coupled with definite realization that some particular good is taking place. (See *Truth is that.*)

prayer, persistence in See *persistence.*

prayer, spiritual communion as See *spiritual communion as prayer.*

prayer, treatment and See *treatment and.*

prayers—some prayers are more effective than others Every prayer is effective in such measure as it creates faith and acceptance. Since one's faith and acceptance more or less vary, it is self-evident that some prayers would be more effective than others.

"precept upon precept, line upon line" Refers to evolution of consciousness.

preconscious Loosely speaking, that part of the memory which is quickly brought to the surface.

premonition Revelation of some future event.

Presence See *God as a Living; God's Presence; One Presence; practicing the Presence; Universal Presence.*

primordial Refers to the First Principle—the Originating Power.

Principle See *over all.*

principle, active and passive See *Universe as a dual.*

Principle always responsive to thought Since Principle is Mind, and thought, or idea, is the only activity of Mind, then the only activity of Principle is the activity of thought, which constitutes the Law of Mind in action. Mind cannot fail to respond to thought.

Principle, Divine See *Divine Principle.*

principle, feminine See *feminine principle.*

Principle, First See *First Principle.*

Principle in action From the standpoint of mental treatment, this means that the treatment sets the Creative Law in motion, which produces a mathematical result.

Principle of Unfoldment The Universal Spirit of Life Itself is the Principle of Unfoldment, for Life is forever evolving, or unfolding higher and higher forms. This Principle is a part of the forward movement of Life, the Nature of Being.

Principle, scientific use of See *scientific use.*

Principle, Self-Knowing See *Self-Knowing Principle.*

Principle—the more it is generalized, the more it can be specialized The more we understand about any law of nature in its universal action, the more definitely we can use it for personal purposes.

principles are universal   Two and two are four here or on the planet Mars. What is true on one plane is true on all. All laws are universal.

problems, working out   Instead of dwelling on the problem, we should recognize its answer, sensing that since the Spirit has no problems, that which appears as a human problem is dissolved and in its place is the right answer.

prophecy   Foreknowing future events.

prophecy, the spirit of   The ability to foreknow what is going to happen; this is not an idea of fate but consists in subconsciously following out a sequence of cause and effect.

prosperity, agency of   See *spiritual communion as an.*

protection, treatment for   See *treatment for.*

prototype   The pattern, or original idea, from which a form is built. An archetype. Spiritual prototypes are the roots of every existing thing.

Providence, no special dispensation of   Neither God nor the Law chose Moses to become a law-giver, or Edison a lightbearer; rather these men chose to specialize the Law. Hence, according to the very law specialized it appears as though a Divine Providence had particularly chosen them. This is in line with the Hermetic saying that nature obeys us as we first obey it, illustrated by Jesus in the washing of the disciples' feet.

psyche   The mental life.

psyche, reeducation of   Reeducation of the whole mental life on a sound foundation of the Unity of God and man.

psychic   One who is able more or less clearly to bring subjective impressions to the surface. Subjective.

psychic body   *Psyche,* from the Greek, means "soul." Thus the psychic body is the vehicle of man, through which he contacts the Soul of the Universe, or the Great Subjective side of Life.

psychic development not necessary for spiritual healing
Since spiritual mind healing is a result of definitely knowing the truth and of making definite statements in Mind, and since psychic development depends largely upon receiving impressions already accepted by oneself or others, it follows that they are two different fields.

psychic life is infused with our own opinions Since the psychic life is largely subjective and also largely partakes of the race consciousness, it is filled with thoughts and opinions of ourselves, of others, and of the race.

psychic revelations Uncovering the subjective life of oneself or others, or of the race consciousness, revealing human, rather than Divine, truths.

psychogenesis Origin and development of the mind. Science of mental development.

psychological adjustments, four great Adjustment to the self, to the family life, to society, and to the Universe.

psychological complex See *complex*.

psychologize Spirit, we don't See *spiritualizing; we neither*.

psychology, relationship to metaphysics Psychology is a study of mental actions and reactions. The Science of Mind, while including individual mental actions and reactions, also assumes a Universal Mind acting and reacting, in and through the individual life.

psychophysics Study of the relationship between body and mind.

psychotherapy From our viewpoint, mental healing.

punishment The inevitable reaction of the Law of Cause and Effect. The destructive use of the law always reacts on the one who uses it.

purify To remove every trace of extraneous matter.

purpose of statements used in mental treatment To convince one's own mind.

purposive accidents Occurrences by which the body suffers injury as a result of circumstances which appear to be fortuitous, but which, in instances, show by their nature that they specifically fulfill unconscious tendencies.

Q

"quench not the Spirit" Be open at all times for inspiration.

R

race belief—each has a tendency to repeat it Thought patterns formed by the consensus of human opinion automatically operate through everyone, unless consciously rejected.

race belief, living under the Living in accord with the law of averages; in accord with what the average person experiences.

race mind The sum total of all human belief throughout the ages. The collective unconscious; race belief; race suggestion. (See *lulled.*)

raising your consciousness Causing one's interior awareness to believe, think, feel, and accept from the standpoint of what one feels spiritual perfection must be.

Real Self The Christ within; the God Principle; the incarnation of the Spirit; the unique individualization of Reality.

Real Self and the counterfeit The Real Self is perfect and eternal; there is no counterfeit other than in belief.

Real Self not evil See *your Real Self.*

Reality See *Divine Reality; religion as.*

Reality back of all creation Spirit of consciousness acting through idea.

Reality back of everything is spiritual There is an invisible cause back of every fact. This cause projects the fact; without it there would be no fact.

Reality is more than an intellectual perception Spiritual truth is something we feel—it is deeper than words—just as we know that we live; it is an interior awareness.

Reality, our world is our view of See *world (our).*

Reality, thought never controls See *thought never.*

realization A complete acceptance of an idea. (See *analytical; intellectual acceptance; intuitional; mental analysis; Truth realized.*)

realization is the healing All mental arguments or processes in spiritual mind healing are for the purpose of creating an interior awareness or state of realization. It is this realization which is the essence of the healing power.

realization, man as See *man as the realization.*

realization—not suggestion but realization See *suggestion —not.*

realization of ideas in the silence Having started communing with the Infinite, one definitely realizes not the need, but its opposite.

realizing the Presence of God Consciously becoming aware
of the Intelligent Perfection at the center of everything.

**receptivity—no one gives to us but ourselves or takes from
us but ourselves** Man is his own heaven and hell;
prayer is its own answer; the law is flowing through each
at the level of his realization of the meaning of life; the
Spirit can only give us what we will take; etc.

reciprocal action By this principle man draws into his experience those conditions and experiences which are in
direct correspondence to that to which his thought is
attuned. It is a part of the Law of Correspondences and
is illustrated by the Hermetic axiom ''As above, so below'' and vice-versa. Thus, if his thought is negative, or
destructive, he finds himself ill or suffering lack, etc. If
his thought is centered in a contemplation of fullness,
abundance, and the joyousness of life, his experience will
be in like nature.

recognition of Substance and Supply The mental acceptance
and realization that Spirit is Substance and that our daily
needs are met through an action of the immutable Law
of Cause and Effect. (See *Substance and Supply; supply.*)

recognition, supreme See *supreme recognition.*

redeem To liberate, or deliver from bondage. To take the
ugly things from the past and transmute them into things
of beauty through treatment. As problems are transmuted
they dissolve, as hate is redeemed (transmuted, or liberated) through love.

Redeemer Spiritual awareness regenerates, transmutes, and
redeems bondage into freedom; pain into pleasure; fear
into faith. (See *our Redeemer.*)

redemption Liberation through at-one-ment with the Christ
Principle; the unity of perfect love and divine wisdom.

Through this Principle our sins (mistakes) are redeemed —that is, liberated, or obliterated.

reflection   See *external world; man as a reflection; soul and; world as.*

reflection never a thing in itself   While the reflection of the image held in front of a mirror reproduces the image as a reflection, it is still never a thing in itself; it is always an effect of the image, while the image is an effect of the consciousness which holds it in place.

reflection of truth   Refers to the thought that what we call the material universe is but a reflection of that which comes under the government of God or Good.

regeneration   A renewal. A new birth on a higher level. The transmutation of disease into health; of any form of limitation into that which is less limited. From the psychological viewpoint it means changing of thought patterns from a basis of confusion to one of harmony with and adjustment to life. From a spiritual viewpoint it means the Second Birth, the spiritual transmutation or purification whereby lower qualities are elevated to spiritual perception.

relative and Absolute   The Absolute is the universal Intelligence and Law, ever giving birth to form. The form is the relative, since its entire existence depends not upon itself, but upon something else. (See *Absolute and.*)

Relative First Cause   See *Cause, Relative First.*

relative may change, the Absolute cannot   All facts and forms are relative. Time, space, and motion are relative. Everything that is created is relative. Relativity is the play of Life upon Itself. Life Itself is an abstract Absolute. It is changeless, but all change takes place within It. It is timeless, yet It gives birth to all time. It is formless, yet It creates all form.

religion Our opinion about God. (See *science and religion; science is; Science of Mind is not a new.*)

religion as an immediate experience of Reality As God is not a person in any restricted sense, but a divine and universal Presence, personified through each one of us and therefore personal to each, so the essence of religion is not a theological or dogmatic belief, but rather an atmosphere of this divine Presence immediately perceived by the individual.

Religious Science A spiritual philosophy which deals with the unity of all life and which proclaims that God Power exists at the center of every person.

"Render unto Caesar the things that are Caesar's" Jesus did not deny conformity with the social systems under which he lived; rather, standing in the midst of these, he proclaimed that the Kingdom of God is at hand.

renewing the mind Creating new images of thought. Thinking from a less limited pattern. (See *transformed.*)

replacing the false belief with the true idea In the practice of spiritual science, we replace all apparent material objects with a spiritual idea. Theoretically, material things are converted into thoughts and the thoughts corrected. Spiritual treatment deals with the destruction of false beliefs. We treat not a person but a belief about the person.

repressed desires unconscious but active Infantile fixations; morbid reactions; painful memories; neurotic sense of guilt: buried in the unconscious, they remain dynamic and active.

"resist not evil" To resist anything is to recognize it. To think of a thing is either to create it or to hold it in place. To resist something is to place it in mind as a genuine obstruction. Hence that which is truly nonresisted by true nonrecognition tends to become displaced.

resolving things into thoughts In mental treatment we theoretically resolve all conditions into thoughts and thus treat all negative conditions as though they were merely false beliefs.

responsibility (personal) in treatment See *personal responsibility.*

resurrection Rising from the belief in death. Rising from the lower to the higher self; from the consciousness of Adam to the realization of Christ. In Christian teaching it refers to the resurrection of Jesus. Psychologically, the sublimation of thought; spiritually, the recognition of Absolute Perfection where imperfection appears to be.

revelation The act of the intellect becoming consciously acquainted with Truth. We believe that this revelation may be a result of subjective accumulation of ideas either in the individual or in the collective unconscious; or it may be a direct impartation of the Universal Mind. Something which the indwelling Spirit of Christ in us reveals to the intellect.

revelation and reason Any alleged revelation which contradicts that which can be proven to be so is not a spiritual revelation but a psychic or subjective hallucination. Revelation can reveal only that which is so.

revelation disguised in symbolism of man's conscious or unconscious desire Refers to a psychological projection; the unconscious operation of one's thought, claiming to be a revelation, but in reality arising out of one's unconscious desire life.

revelation of truth The intuitive perception of what is so.

revelation, personal opinions masquerading as Our own unconscious thoughts, desires, motivations, etc., appearing to us as divine revelations.

revelation, Science of Mind is not See *Science of Mind is not a revelation.*

revelations, false Derived from the consciousness of individuals or collections of individuals, but with no relationship to Truth itself.

Reversal, Law of See *Law of Reversal.*

reversal of thought, conscious By denying certain false assumptions, the practitioner reverses their effects, just as one would pull up weeds in a garden.

reversing our negatives Replacing negative thoughts with their opposites, or positive thoughts.

reversing our use of the Law To break down old thought patterns and impose new ones, thus consciously causing a new sequence of cause and effect in the individual experience.

reward Refers to the Law of Cause and Effect automatically bringing to each an objective manifestation of his subjective thoughts and actions.

reward and punishment The Law of Cause and Effect in action.

right ideas To transpose material objects into their spiritual equivalents; this does not deny the object but affirms its spiritual cause.

right ideas, activity of Correct ideas have the power not only to destroy that which appears to oppose them but to establish themselves in our experience as concrete facts.

right ideas destroy false beliefs Just as the knowledge that two and two make four dissipates a belief that two and two make five, so a deep, inner spiritual realization of harmony dissipates evil.

right ideas enforce the Law of Mind Clear thinking based upon the proposition that Spirit constitutes the right ideas which use the Law of Cause and Effect for specific purposes. This is scientific practice.

right ideas, power of As light overcomes darkness, so statements of truth neutralize that which contradicts them.

right knowing To correctly sense the relationship between the universal "I Am" and the individualized "I." Man as a reflection, a manifestation, an embodiment, an incarnation, or as the off-spring of God—whichever term one may choose to use—can be nothing other than God's idea of Himself reflected in man. To realize this relative to any apparent negation is right knowing.

right thinking, achievement through The objective manifestation which automatically follows changes of thought.

righteousness The quality of being right, honest. One is righteous who acts from a sense of justice. He performs right action because he could not act from any other principle.

"Rise, take up thy bed and walk" Supremacy of Spirit over all material objects.

"Rock whence ye are hewn" Man is some part of the Great Creative Principle; he is the spiritual likeness of Its eternal self-existence.

S

salt of the earth Symbolic of Divine wisdom, purity, and goodness.

salvation Conscious realization of the omnipresence of Spirit.

Perception of our unity with good, resulting in those acts which conform to the eternal verities. The discovery that good known and embodied destroys apparent evil.

salvation already achieved In Science of Mind we realize that truth already is; we discover and use it.

salvation, now is the day of Refers to the idea that salvation comes when we recognize it as belonging to us, when we claim it. Since time is but an experience within that which of itself is timeless, and since time exists for us only through the act of experience, and since past time no longer exists although it has left a record of itself, and since future time has no existence other than as a tendency, it follows that only where attention is placed can there be experience, and attention can be placed only in the here and now. All treatment must be given in the present tense, since Law knows neither past nor future.

Satan Symbolic of darkness, relativity, limitation, and ignorance. (See *"Get thee."*)

Saviour The true saviour is the recognition of the Supreme Spirit as All in all. (See *"I am the Lord . . . Beside"; inner Saviour; Jesus Christ; knowing the Truth is the Saviour; serpent and.*)

science Pertaining to spiritual truth, a systematic knowledge of spiritual laws. (See *Divine Science.*)

science and opinion Science is a systematized knowledge of laws and therefore must be accurate; opinion is one's belief about something and therefore may or may not be true.

science and religion A knowledge of natural laws and causes both in the mental and in the physical world, coupled with a consciousness of the spiritual Presence in everything.

science is a study of the mechanics of the universe; religion is a study of values   Every science, including the Science of Mind, is a study of exact mathematical laws, while religion seeks to use these laws in moral, ethical, and spiritual ways.

science of being   The Law of Mind and Spirit governing man's relationship to the spiritual universe.

science of God-Power   Knowledge of the creative power of thought governed by love and wisdom.

science of love   The mathematical necessity that thoughts of love shall heal fear, hate, confusion, etc.

Science of Mind   Science of the laws of thought as they pertain to man's relationship to the universal creative Mind and to health, happiness, and success.

Science of Mind is not a new religion   It may be added to any spiritual system of thought and is a complement to all.

Science of Mind is not a revelation   Like other sciences, the Science of Mind is worked out as intuition guides personal intelligence to an understanding of the laws of cause and effect. This science is not only mental, it is also spiritual. The highest use of the laws of Mind is based upon spiritual perceptions which include love, unity, and conscious fellowship with the Invisible.

sciences are impersonal   Any science is a study of natural laws which respond impersonally to whoever uses them.

scientific attitude for a spiritual practitioner   To know that God is all there is, that truth known demonstrates itself; to know that what one knows is the truth and therefore must be effective.

scientific Christian   One who definitely practices the Law of Mind from the motivation of the precepts laid down by Jesus.

scientific prayer Conscious use of spiritual power for definite purposes.

scientific silence Consciously withdrawing from contemplation of external facts, conditions, etc., to the quiet realization that truth is governing.

scientific use of the Mind Principle Treatment is definite, directed for specific purposes, conscious, and always carries with it a definite intention.

sea A symbol of the mental plane uncontrolled by Spirit, over which Jesus walked, into which Jonah fell, and through which the Children of Israel were symbolically led by Moses, whose spiritual power parted the waters of mental confusion.

seamless robe of Truth The unity of all life represented by the garment made from one piece of cloth.

"Search the scriptures, for in them ye think ye have eternal life" Eternal Life does not exist in a book, in a religion, or in a philosophy. These may tell about it, but the Kingdom of God is within.

secondary cause See *cause, secondary*.

"See that no man know it" Do not subject your faith to the confusion of another person's doubt.

"Seek ye first the Kingdom of God" Turn completely to Absolute Causation, which contains all possible effects.

seen comes from the unseen Everything we see and experience in the objective world has an identical correspondent in the subjective and spiritual world, which is its cause.

self The center of God consciousness having awareness. (See *Real Self*.)

Self-Approval, Law of See *Law of Self-Approval.*

self-choice Refers to individuality, selectivity, personal decision.

self-condemnation It is unscientific to condemn oneself or others.

self-hood, your true See *your true.*

Self-Knowing Mind The conscious mind.

Self-Knowing Principle Spiritual treatment operates in a field of mind, which, acting as Law, knows how to convert the treatment into conditions.

self-realization To realize one's unity with the God-Self, and hence unity with Life Itself and with all that is. Inner acknowledgment and understanding of the spiritual truth of one's being.

self-treatment Inner awareness of spiritual perfection for one's own self.

sending out thoughts Refers to the mistaken idea that a spiritual mind practitioner sends out thoughts.

sense the power back of your word; do not try to put power into it It is our realization of Power which makes the word effective, but the Power exists before we use It; we do not create It.

separate discordant mental beliefs and discordant physical conditions from the idea of spiritual man The spiritual practitioner assumes that both mental and physical discord are never things in themselves; they do not belong to the Real Man. This does not deny, however, that they are real enough as experiences.

separateness A belief in duality which gives rise to the thought that we are separated from God, therefore from Good.

separating the belief from the believer In spiritual mind healing we seek to realize that a false condition does not belong to anyone, has no law to support it and no existence in reality, hence need not have any existence in fact.

Sequence, Law of See *Law of Sequence.*

sequence of causation Starts with pure Intelligence; movement of intelligence, which is intelligence becoming aware of something. The Law of Mind set in motion by consciousness, followed by the objective manifestation, or the demonstration. (See *Cause and Effect, sequence; mental law is.*)

series of treatments Repeated statements of truth for some person or condition over a period of time.

serpent Symbolic of the Life Principle.

serpent and saviour The Life Principle viewed from the Adam or isolated consciousness, or the Christ or unified consciousness. Refers to the Life Principle viewed materialistically, which produces bondage, or viewed idealistically—that is, in conscious union with Spirit, which produces salvation. The serpent is symbolic of the Life Principle. Crawling flat upon the face of the earth, it becomes the Life Principle viewed as disunion, separation, evil, etc. This same Life Principle lifted upon the cross—that is, elevated to a realization of unity—becomes the Saviour.

serpent in the Garden of Eden Typifies the Life Principle viewed from a merely materialistic viewpoint. The serpent which Moses lifted up in the wilderness refers to the Life Principle elevated above the materialistic viewpoint.

serpent lifted up in the wilderness The Life Principle viewed as a spiritual principle. (See above.)

serpent with tail in its mouth The Life Principle viewed as without beginning and without end.

servant of the Spirit Refers to the Law of Mind in action.

shepherd Symbolizes the Higher Self ever drawing our experience into conformity with divine union.

shield of faith A positive thought of complete conviction.

silence, going into the Withdrawing the thought from external things and mentally dwelling upon a realization of the Divine Presence. It is from this center that Spiritual Power proceeds.

silence, purpose of the To still mental action, thus holding consciousness in an expectant and receptive attitude toward the Divine Influx.

silence, scientific See *scientific silence.*

silver cord, the See *"Or ever."*

simplicity in treatment All treatments should be stated in the simplest possible manner. In this way they will be more meaningful to the one making the statements, and therefore the statements will have more power.

sin—"Neither hath this man sinned nor his parents" Neither the possibility of having lived before and having carried the liabilities of such a life into this world as bad Karma, nor inherited tendencies, affect the Real Man.

"Sin no more lest a worse thing come unto thee" If we continue in our old sins or mistakes, we shall not only continue to project them, but the projection will continually become multiplied as the intensity of thought back of the projection becomes increased.

sin, whosoever committeth sin is the servant of We are caught in our own thought patterns; if they are sinful or mistaken thought patterns, they bind us until we neutralize them. "Therefore if the Son shall make you free, ye shall be free indeed."

single eye, the Refers to the inner vision which must be in tune with Light; then is the body filled with light. Thought processes must be inspired by Truth rather than evil.

"So shall my word be . . . it shall not return unto me void" Man's spiritual awareness must produce a result; it must demonstrate.

"soft answer (a) turneth away wrath" To meet evil with evil is to perpetuate it; to meet evil with good is to destroy the evil while the good remains.

Son See *Beloved Son; Father (the) and; Only-Begotten Son.*

"Son of man is Lord even of the sabbath" Our use of things is what makes them holy; they are not holy in themselves.

soul and its reflection This means that cause and effect are the same thing.

soul, animal Symbolic representation of thought in reference to physical life.

soul, human Thoughts and emotions about family, friends, life in general, etc.

soul, journey of the Refers to the cycle of experience through which the ego passes on the pathway of self-discovery.

soul of the universe Refers to the Universal Subjectivity.

soul, spiritual Upper reaches of self-awareness; contemplation of God, Reality, etc.

space The apparent nothingness which separates one object from another. That which is created by motion.

specific treatment If we wish definite results we must be definite in treatment.

spiral, eternal upward A theory that in the evolution of the soul the individual ego continuously repeats former experiences in an ascending scale.

Spirit Life essence which permeates all persons and all things. The Thing within everything which makes it what it is. God, the Living Spirit Almighty. (See *One Body.*)

Spirit and the material universe There is no material universe other than Spirit in form.

Spirit appears wherever recognized Since the Life Principle is omnipresent, It springs into being wherever we recognize It. To see God, Life, Power in anything is to cause that thing to respond in like manner.

Spirit, approaching the See *faith—approaching.*

Spirit as knower and Law as doer does not imply duality Just as the engineer is not to be confused with the engine, so the Self-Knowing Mind is not to be confused with the mathematical and mechanical subjective reactions.

Spirit breathes Itself into form The Self-realization of God produces creation.

Spirit ever available We contact the Spirit within our own thought, hence we are never separated from It.

Spirit, God is See *God is Spirit.*

Spirit inspires and the Law obeys Through intuition we are inspired from on High. The Law of Mind automatically reacts to our thought patterns.

Spirit is both Cause and Effect Once the creative word is spoken, the effect must follow. The mental practitioner bases his assurance upon this—i.e., a silent recognition of the Truth within his own consciousness must produce an inevitable result wherever and for whatsoever purpose such consciousness is directed. (See *Truth is both.*)

Spirit is form-giving, but subjective law is form-taking The conscious mind decides, and the subjective law must react upon this decision with mathematical precision as well as with creative power.

Spirit is personal to each one of us Since each is a center of God Consciousness, the Spirit must be personal where It is personified. There is an Infinite Self back of every apparent finite self.

Spirit is self-propelling All energy is within Spirit.

Spirit is the realm of causation, form is the realm of effect All causation is invisible; the objective world is the effect of an invisible cause which exactly corresponds to it.

Spirit—"not by power nor by might, but by Spirit" This means that we do not labor with the Law or with the Lord; rather by silent contemplation, recognizing the supremacy of good, it becomes manifest in our experience.

Spirit of God, Law of Mind confused with See *superstition.*

"Spirit (the) of God moved upon the face of the waters" Symbolizes the movement of idea upon mind.

Spirit of His Spirit Man's spirit is the Spirit of God in man. The two are one.

"Spirit (the) of man is the candle of the Lord" Refers to the "I Am" which is the light of the world; the Celestial Flame incarnated at the Center of every man's being.

Spirit of Truth Refers to the divine Presence which both indwells and overshadows everything, which Spirit is Truth and which Truth is Spirit. It might also refer to our conscious contact with Reality.

Spirit ordains perfection Since it is the nature of Spirit to be perfect, and since Its law reflects Its nature, then Spirit can ordain only perfection.

Spirit, Originating See *Originating.*

Spirit, servant of the See *servant.*

Spirit, Sword of See *Sword.*

Spirit that quickeneth, it is the Real life is from within out, hence the flesh profiteth nothing. That is not a denial of the flesh but rather an affirmation that it is an effect and not a cause.

Spirit, Walk in See *"Walk."*

spirits, discarnate See *discarnate.*

spirits, evil See *evil spirits.*

spirits—"Try the spirits whether they are of God" The apostle is telling us not to believe in every alleged spiritual communication. He tells us to beware of mistaking what today we call psychic hallucinations for spiritual revelations. At the doorway of the psychic life he would put up a sign: *Stop, Look, and Listen.*

spiritual The atmosphere of God in human consciousness.

spiritual adjustment Elevating the mental adjustment to the consciousness that all things are unified with God.

spiritual affirmations Affirming the Allness of Truth, Spirit, Love, etc.

spiritual body We do not deny body, we merely affirm that it is spiritual. Body constitutes the evidence of Mind. The spiritual body is perfect; it is a body of right ideas.

spiritual communion Inwardly sensing Reality as life, love, beauty, truth, divine Presence, etc.

spiritual communion as a healing agency Inwardly sensing Reality followed by a definite knowing that this Reality is manifest rather than the disease. This might call for a certain amount of affirmation and denial.

spiritual communion as an agency of prosperity Inwardly sensing the Divine as perfect substance, forever taking the form of successful action in one's affairs.

spiritual communion as prayer Spiritual communion itself is not a prayer or petition, so much as it is an announcement of the presence of Reality.

spiritual conception in healing When the practitioner's consciousness recognizes the Truth, the healing work is accomplished.

Spiritual Demonstration, Law of See *Law of Spiritual Demonstration.*

spiritual dominion The power to govern our lives through silent realization of inner spiritual power.

spiritual ethers Just as physical energy is born out of the ethers of physics, so mental energy is born out of the ethers of Spirit.

spiritual expectation To be continuously expectant of and receptive to that which is good, beautiful, and true.

spiritual experience Conscious inner awareness of the Divine Presence as Reality, Law, and Order.

spiritual feeling An inner sense of the Presence of Spirit which produces a psychological reaction not only of acceptance, but of warmth and color.

spiritual healer as an agent The spiritual practitioner, recognizing the Divine Power, becomes a transmitter through which It flows in the direction he indicates.

spiritual healing See *healing; spiritual mind healing; theory; treatment.*

spiritual healing, basis of A realization of spiritual body, spiritual perfection, perfect action, and perfect reaction.

spiritual healing, chief emphasis in Realization of the perfection, the unity, and the omnipresence of Life.

spiritual healing, conscious mind is the actor in Spiritual mind healing is not a result of receiving psychic or subjective impressions; it is always conscious, active, and specific. The conscious acts, the subconscious reacts.

spiritual healing, impersonal When one's consciousness is subjectively charged with Truth, it automatically radiates life, and anyone coming near that person receives benefit, just as did the woman who touched the hem of the robe of Jesus.

spiritual healing—it is the psychological and the physical man who needs healing Spiritual mind healing is based on the assumption that Spirit is already perfect, that Mind is the creative factor, and that body conditions are effects. The physician treats the body, the psychologist and metaphysician treat the mind. There need be no confusion over this.

spiritual identity The inner and ever-increasing recognition of one's relationship to Spirit in one's identity in Mind. Refers to the individualized center of God Consciousness, which is a unique presentation of the Christ Spirit within each one of us.

spiritual insight Deeper than intellectual conviction; inward experience of Reality.

spiritual insight and enlightenment The knowledge that we are One with the Great Self and that which is experienced is merely a reflection or manifestation of Being.

spiritual mind healing See *healing; spiritual healing; theory; treatment.*

spiritual mind healing is the result of clear thinking This is true both psychologically and metaphysically. It could not be true in either case unless there were a perfect Principle to be demonstrated. Since this Principle is Mind and Spirit, and since the activity of Mind and Spirit is conscious, it follows that consciousness is the thing that needs to be straightened out.

spiritual mind healing, premise underlying Perfect God, Perfect Man, and Perfect Being.

spiritual mind practitioner One who uses the Law of Mind and Spirit in behalf of others. (See *practitioner.*)

spiritual plane The mental plane elevated to spiritual awareness. It is the mind that must become conscious, hence intuition and reality must operate through consciousness to be known. This knowing is sometimes merely pure feeling without processes of thought, but it is always awareness.

spiritual power released through thinking Spiritual power is also mental power, and since thought is the only activity of mind, it is the only thing that can release spiritual power. Spiritual power, like electrical energy, exists in the universe. So far as we are concerned, it exists on a certain level of thought, consciousness, or inward comprehension. In such degree as one reaches this inward comprehension, this power is released through his word for purposes which his intention designates. (See *only those.*)

spiritual prototype The universal idea back of any particular form. For example: the abstract idea of Beauty back of the beautiful.

spiritual psychology The study of mental actions and reactions and the reeducation of the mind through introducing new and spiritual patterns of thought.

spiritual realities The invisible essence of things. The proto-type in the invisible world of that which is visible.

spiritual science Knowledge of the Laws of Spirit.

spiritual science, application of Conscious use of the Laws of Spirit as they operate in and through man and human affairs.

spiritual sense substituted for physical objects In spiritual mind healing we think of the different physical functions as being spiritual activities of a perfect body and treat to realize the perfection of the spiritual, which realization in its turn reflects itself into the physical.

spiritual sleep A lack of spiritual enlightenment.

spiritual thanksgiving Joyous acceptance and gratitude.

spiritual therapy From our viewpoint, spiritual mind healing.

spiritual things must be spiritually discerned If we would understand the universe as a spiritual system, our own consciousness must become spiritualized, raised, or elevated to the perception of a spiritual universe. With this perception the spiritual universe will immediately be-come real to us.

spiritual treatment Applying the law of the Christ Mind to human problems. (See *mental spiritual; practitioner; treat; treating; treatment.*)

spiritual understanding An inner awareness of the Presence of God in all people and in all things.

spiritual universe The universe as a spiritual system gov-erned by the Laws of Mind. The Real Universe. The only true universe, which includes what we call the physical.

spiritual universe is apparent through the physical The

Emersonian concept that the physical universe consists of thought in form and that the laws of nature are identical with the laws of thought.

spiritual values added to psychology Realization that all mental actions and reactions are a result not merely of environmental or inherited stimuli, but also of the Divine Urge inherent in the nature of being.

spiritual victory The transcendent power of spiritual thought forces over apparent material or physical resistance, which an inner awareness of God inevitably demonstrates.

spiritual vision Perceiving the eternal Presence and Wholeness, Truth and Beauty in every person and in every thing.

spiritual wholeness is not evolving Spiritual wholeness is already a fact. As the principle of mathematics must be applied from the understanding of its absoluteness, so the spiritual mind practitioner must apply his Principle from the viewpoint of the instantaneous availablity of Wholeness.

spiritualizing matter We neither spiritualize matter nor psychologize Spirit in mental healing; we know the truth about being, which truth known automatically demonstrates itself. (See *we neither.*)

"Stand fast therefore in the liberty wherewith Christ hath made us free and be not entangled again with the yoke of bondage" This means keep the vision of Truth and Unity and do not again believe in the reality of separation.

Star of Bethlehem Inner guidance.

still small voice See *God in the.*

stream of consciousness The automatic mental emanation of the subjective state of thought.

streams of consciousness, tuning into Any mental state which we assume tunes into corresponding states in the race consciousness, tending to draw similar states into our own thought.

strong in the Lord Strong in the realization of the invisible Power.

subconscious denial of our affirmations The thought content of the subconscious mind refusing to accept a conscious affirmation. This, of course, can be changed.

subconscious does not mean unconscious The subconscious, whether we think of it as individual or universal (for the two are one), must receive images of thought as they are created, without choice or volition of its own; but having received these images of thought, it operates upon them intelligently.

subconscious intelligence Intelligence operating upon patterns of thought creatively and intelligently without reflective or self-conscious knowing.

subjective acceptance The subconscious no longer denying what the conscious mind has affirmed.

subjective metaphysics Telepathy, clairvoyance, etc.

Subjective Mind as mechanical law Thought, falling into a subjective state, enters into a mechanical field of cause and effect.

subjective mind, our The use we make of the One Law. There is but One Mind which we all use; but One Law of Mind which we all employ. What we call our subjective mind is merely our mental reaction in the One Law of Mind.

subjective mind, our: as a point in Universal Mind There is only one Subjective Mind, which everyone uses; what we call our subjective mind is merely a reaction of this

Universal Subjectivity to our thought. Hence it is not individual but may become individualized.

subjective molds This refers to the habitual thought patterns which are in the subconscious mind.

subjective side of life The invisible Law of Cause and Effect, which operates upon our images of thought.

subjective state of thought, changing the The subjective thought is the medium between the Absolute and the relative in our experience; it works automatically, mathematically, and mechanically, but it is entirely a created thing. Hence it can be changed through conscious thinking.

subjective unity between all people Just as there is but One Spirit and One Mind, so there is but One Psyche or Soul or Subjectivity. It is because of this that such phenomena as clairvoyance, telepathy, etc., may function.

subjective world The world of causes.

subjective world as cause of the objective There is a spiritual or mental likeness or equivalent in the invisible world for every objective fact. It also follows that wherever the spiritual or mental equivalent or image is provided, an objective fact must follow.

sublimation, law of Transforming one type of energy into another.

sublimation of thought To convert desire into pure, perfect, and wholesome channels of self-expression.

subliminal consciousness The impersonal self; that which lies beneath the level of the conscious mind. The subconsciousness. It is the vehicle for certain psychic phenomena, such as clairvoyance, clairaudience, automatic writing, etc.

subliminal mind That realm of thought which functions in conscious union with Spirit. The Christ Mind.

submission This is not to a greater force, but to a higher intelligence.

Substance The Formless, from which all forms are created. (See *faith—Substance.*)

Substance and Supply The eternal Creative Spirit as Substance is everywhere taking the form of those desires which we affirm, believe in, and embody. Mind gives us ideas; ideas project the Law into form. (See *recognition; supply.*)

Substance and Supply, recognition of The mental acceptance and realization that Spirit is Substance and that our daily needs are met through an action of the immutable Law of Cause and Effect.

success Fulfillment of legitimate constructive desires. Any form of satisfactory self-expression which harms no other person.

suggestion(s) See *collective negative suggestions.*

suggestion—not suggestion but realization Spiritual mind treatment is not mental suggestion. That is, the practitioner does not suggest anything to the patient. The practitioner seeks to realize something for the patient within his, the practitioner's, own consciousness. (See *we neither; thought, clarify.*)

super-mind faculties Abilities of spiritual thought to discern invisible truths as being equal (real) with objective facts.

supernatural That which lies beyond the realm of the natural, or the understandable on the material plane. That which cannot be explained by physical laws.

superstition and ignorance confuse the Law of Mind with the Spirit of God The Law of Mind is like any other law in nature. It is a dynamic and creative Intelligence responding to thought and should not be confused with the Spirit of God, which is a universal Self-Knowingness, or with the spirit of man, which is an individualized center of this Self-Knowingness.

Supply See *Substance and.*

supply as a spiritual idea To recognize that invisible Mind and Substance are ever taking the forms which meet our daily needs. (See *invisible supply.*)

supply, ideas of: enforce the law of Substance Substance, or the possibility of all right action, forever exists. The Law of Supply is the result of a conscious recognition of this Substance taking definite form. (See *recognition; Substance and Supply.*)

supply—the greater the demand, the more abundant The universal creative Law knows nothing of big or little; It meets our demands by reflecting them back into form. Hence, the more complete the demand, the more complete the reflection. The whole process is automatic.

supply, treating for See *treating.*

suppositional opposite to Truth Any belief which denies the allness of Creative Love, Wisdom, and Power.

supreme affirmation Any mental attitude which affirms its complete unity with God. A recognition that the universal "I Am" and the individualized "I" constitute one being.

supreme recognition Recognizing the presence of pure and perfect Spirit.

surrender This does not mean surrendering the intellect or the personal integrity; it means the necessity of understanding that laws work for us only as we first obey them. As Hermes said, "Nature obeys us as we first obey it."

Sustaining Infinite We are surrounded by, immersed in, and there is within us, the Principle of pure Spirit and perfect Law.

Sword of Spirit The word of Truth.

Sword of Spirit which is the Word of God A definite constructive statement made in Mind can specifically neutralize, sever as it were, any opposite destructive belief.

T

talking to God Communion with the inner Self—for it is only at the center of one's own being that he meets the universal Presence which is forever individualized through him.

teaching without practice It is useless to assume to be a teacher in this Science without practicing it. One soon tends to deal merely with theories and not with actual experience. We know only what we can do. Merely to theorize never proves any principle. It is the practical application of this Mind Principle which alone demonstrates Its reality or our understanding of It.

temple See *"Lord is in."*

Tendency, Law of See *Law of Tendency.*

thanksgiving See *praise; pray with; spiritual thanksgiving.*

"That which is born of the flesh is flesh; and that which is born of the Spirit is Spirit" Jesus definitely recognized more than one plane for self-expression. Every plane of being has laws common to its own functioning. The higher form of intelligence governs the lower, therefore that which is born of the Spirit controls that which is born of the flesh.

theology Any religious system of thought. The critical, historical, and psychological study of religion and religious ideas.

theory upon which technique of spiritual mind healing is based Perfection; unity of God with man; Oneness of all Life; Perfect Being; perfect manifestation.

"there is no power against me" In so far as we believe in the One and only Power, there can be no contradiction to It or manifestation different from It.

there is nothing but mind and what mind does The Mind Principle is both the unformed and the formed. Creation is Mind passing into form, just as ice is water in form. (See *nothing but.*)

"There is nothing covered that shall not be revealed" All things are known to Mind.

"There is that that scattereth, and yet increaseth" As a seed, scattered, drops into the soil and in reproduction multiplies itself, so right thoughts and constructive acts both reproduce and multiply themselves.

"There is therefore no condemnation to them which are in Christ Jesus" Where the light is, there is no darkness; where peace abides, confusion has fled.

"They that take up the sword shall perish with the sword" Refers to the Law of Cause and Effect.

"They that wait upon the Lord shall renew their strength" An inner awareness of Spirit renews the whole being.

"They think that they shall be heard for their much speaking" The power of a mental treatment lies not in the type or number of words used in a statement, but in one's sense of their meaning.

Thing Itself, the God, Spirit, Reality.

Thinker (the) alone is ultimate and absolute the movement of consciousness within itself is the starting point of all creation.

thinking center in Mind The individual mind is a conscious, volitional, and spontaneous center of self-awareness, which self-awareness operating through mind acts as law.

"This kind can come forth by nothing but by prayer and fasting" Deep-rooted unbelief is cast out only through consecration, meditation, faith, and realization. Prayer means completely to accept, while fasting means completely to refrain from dwelling on the negative.

"Thou . . . canst not look on iniquity" God sees only perfection, and to the pure all is pure.

thought Movement of consciousness. (See *faith is a thing; faithful.*)

thought can undo what thought has done In spiritual mind healing we theoretically resolve things into thoughts and states of consciousness. Next we neutralize by denial or through affirmation those states of consciousness which are not conducive to harmony. Thus we erase, or sublimate, or transform, or convert the old thought patterns into new ones which are now elevated to the point of spiritual comprehension. (See *thought—what.*)

thought, changing the subjective state of See *subjective state.*

thought, clarify your own In spiritual treatment one does not suggest anything to another; he is alone with his sense of Reality, clarifying his own thought about the person or the condition he wishes to help.

thought control This does not mean controlling the thoughts of another; it means controlling one's own thinking.

thought controls our destiny, it does not control the cosmos
It is fortunate that this is so, else our thought would destroy the cosmos. Man is a microcosm within a macrocosm and fortunately has the privilege of controlling only himself.

thought, faithful in See *faithful.*

thought, food for See *food for.*

thought moves as mechanical but intelligent law Thought, which is spontaneous, is operated upon by the Law, which is intelligent but has no consciousness—that is, no self-realization that it is operating. This law is the Law of Cause and Effect.

thought, neutralizing See *neutralizing.*

thought never controls Reality Our thought does not control Reality; it merely interprets It. For instance, we do not control the concept that two and two make four; however, thought uses the mental law for specific purposes.

thought processes as action Spiritual science views the processes of mind or thought as constituting the only ultimate action, therefore mind in action becomes law.

thought, sublimation of See *sublimation of.*

thought, tools of All thoughts are tools from the standpoint of operating in Mind with mathematical precision. Different kinds of thoughts become different kinds of tools. For example, the thought of circulation establishes circulation; the thought of want condenses into the idea of limitation, and thoughts of freedom produce freedom; etc.

thought, transformation of See *transformation.*

thought, unconscious See *unconscious.*

thought—what thought has done thought can undo If this were not true, neither metaphysical nor psychological work would be effective; both rest on the assumption that mental actions can be changed, therefore mental reactions can be changed. (See *thought can*.)

thoughts are things Thoughts are things in the sense that thought is like an image held in front of a mirror—the reflection in the mirror is the thing or the effect.

thoughts—do not hold them, release them The office of a mental treatment is not to hold a thought, but to loose an idea into action.

thoughts, resolving things into See *resolving*.

thoughts, sending See *sending*.

thoughts, transforming power of See *transforming*.

thoughts, we heal See *we heal*.

"Thy faith hath made thee whole" Positive acceptance demonstrates its own realization according to cause and effect. Inward belief and acceptance externalized as outward fact.

"Thy Father which seeth in secret shall reward thee openly" The Law of Mind and Spirit is invisible, but when we use It, It produces a visible result.

"Thy maker is thine husband" There is complete partnership between the universal and the individual.

"Thy sins be forgiven thee" All mistakes of the past are wiped away; today is a fresh beginning.

"Thy will be done" Since the Will of God and the Nature of God are identical, ''Thy Will be done'' means ''I recognize the Nature of Reality and permit It to operate in my experience—I accept it.'' (See *Will of God*.)

time Any sequence of events. Any measure of experience. That which is created by attention.

time and eternity Time is any sequence of events in a unitary wholeness. Eternity means the possibility of endless sequences of experience.

"To whom ye yield yourselves, servants, to obey, his servants ye are" Means that we are like what we think.

"Today shalt thou be with me in paradise" According to the philosophy of Jesus, the transition from this life into the next is immediate.

trance medium One who puts himself in a subjective state in the performance of his work as a medium.

transcend the condition as it actually exists A spiritual practitioner theoretically resolves things into thoughts and conditions into states of mind. Thus limitation becomes an idea which must be transcended in consciousness.

transformation of thought Changing thought patterns from a negative to a positive basis, or from a belief in evil to a belief in or realization of good.

transformed by renewing the mind The instantaneous or gradual process of consciously changing thought patterns until the subconscious surrenders its old patterns for the new. Changing subjective thought patterns by supplying spiritual ideas creates new conditions in body and affairs.

transforming power of thoughts and words The magic power of renewing the mind through affirmations of unity and strength; of faith instead of fear; etc.

translating the false into the true By mentally reversing a false statement, we automatically declare its opposite, which is truth, thus announcing that truth is all there is.

transpose the physical condition In spiritual mind healing one theoretically transposes all physical conditions into their mental and spiritual equivalents. For instance, brain would be the capacity to think, eyes the idea of vision; etc.

treasures in heaven, to lay up   Since Jesus has already defined the Kingdom of Heaven as an interior state of spiritual awareness, to lay up treasures in heaven must mean to bring the intellect or the conscious processes of thought into alignment with spiritual truth.

treat   See *mental treatment; spiritual treatment; treat; treatment.*

treat in the present tense   Mind knows neither past nor future, therefore treatment must always be in the now.

treat to know   Work until your entire mental response is affirmative, until you arrive at a conclusion of realization.

treating   See *mental treatment; spiritual treatment; treat; treatment.*

treating for supply   The spiritual realization that Substance as supply is meeting every need. Conscious recognition of Divine guidance, Divine protection, and limitless Abundance.

treating in the Absolute   Mentally turning entirely from any condition as an effect to pure Spirit as Absolute Cause, without processes of reasoning or mental argument. Seeking a complete inner realization of the Divine Presence. Of course the intention of the practitioner is that such a realization shall benefit the person he seeks to help. (See *Absolute, the.*)

treating nerves   See *nerves.*

treating pain   See *pain.*

treatment   See pp. 154–157; *acceptance; body of right; declare; denial; disease as; healing; intellectual acceptance; meditation with; mental spiritual; mental treatment; neutralize fear; never too late; no one; one place; power of a; practitioner; realization; resolving; scientific use; separate; series; spiritual sense; spiritual treatment; treat; treating; word does; words.*

treatment a definite statement in mind Mental treatment consists of definite thoughts consciously used for specific purposes, based on the assumption that there is a Mind Principle which executes them.

treatment, absent Treatment where the one being helped is at a physical distance from the practitioner.

treatment, affirmation in See *affirmation in.*

treatment, alone with God in The spiritual practitioner does not hold thoughts, suggest, coerce, will, concentrate mind, or do anything other than convince himself of the supremacy of Good. He works alone in his own thought no matter whom he is working for, or for what purpose his treatment is given.

treatment and prayer Prayer is the communion with the spiritual Presence, and often a petition to the Divine Intelligence. Treatment is a recognition of the Divine Presence at the center of everything, and a realization that the Law of Cause and Effect is creatively set in motion through conscious thought and direction.

treatment, clarify your thought in See *thought, clarify.*

treatment, directing See *directing your treatment.*

treatment, do not hold thoughts in See *thoughts—do not.*

treatment for protection Inner realization or awareness of one's immunity from evil.

treatment—in spiritual mind treatment it is not necessary to know the specific cause of the discord one wishes to heal Unlike analytical psychology, which must uncover the specific cause of the neurosis, spiritual mind healing, through the use of broad generalized statements, produces the same effect.

treatment is a law unto itself Every mental and spiritual treatment specializes the One universal creative law, causing It to flow in the direction designated in the treatment and for the purpose specified by the treatment. Thus each treatment individualizes the universal Law in a unique way and becomes a law unto itself through the one Law.

treatment is conscious and spontaneous, whereas the Law reacts automatically Spiritual mind treatment is a definite act of consciousness functioning through volition or self-choice. Everything that happens to the treatment after it is given is in a field of mechanical law. Thus it is done unto us as we believe.

treatment is cumulative Each treatment, consisting of a set of statements, helps to create a subjective or complete mental acceptance. When this subjective, as well as conscious, state of acceptance is entirely in the affirmative, a demonstration is made. The time element involved in this may be what we call of short or long duration. The absolute time element involved is in comparison only with the degree of recognition and realization obtained.

treatment is good when the practitioner knows it is good It is conscious belief, faith, and conviction that one's word, operating through law, is power, which gives power to it.

treatment, mental: is more than a mechanical process The mechanics of a mental treatment consist of the words and ideas used. These words and ideas, however, must be clothed upon with the living consciousness of Spirit.

treatment—mentally knowing the Truth is a spiritual treatment Since knowing the Truth is an act of thought or consciousness, it follows that consciously knowing the Truth is correct application of the Principle in practice. (See *knowing the Truth is treatment.*)

treatment, metaphysical A system of spiritual realization for oneself or some other person.

treatment must be independent of circumstances Treating in the Absolute without reference to any existing condition. The understanding that a treatment creates new conditions or remolds old ones without in any way being limited by them.

treatment must contain a sense of fulfillment Since the power of a treatment is the conviction back of the words, it follows that this conviction must arrive at a sense of fulfillment before the treatment is complete. Since nothing can come out of a treatment unless it is first put in, it follows that the result of a treatment will exactly equal the realization generated in the act of giving treatment.

treatment, no physical sensation in Mental treatment is entirely an act of the mind. Although a certain emotional content may be aroused by realization, physical sensation, as such, is no part of the treatment.

treatment, outlining in See *outlining.*

treatment, personal responsibility and obligation in See *personal responsibility.*

treatment, power of See *power of.*

treatment, present Treatment where the one being helped is in the physical presence of the practitioner.

treatment, purpose of statements in See *purpose.*

treatment, self- See *self-treatment.*

treatment, silent A mental treatment given in one's own thought; not audibly spoken.

treatment, simplicity in See *simplicity.*

treatment—theory on which based See *theory.*

treatment—there is nothing occult or mysterious about mental treatment No peculiar psychic, occult, or hidden powers are necessary in spiritual mind healing. There is no mystery about it; it has a definite Principle to demonstrate and a definite technique to use. Anyone may understand it.

treatment, to know is Conscious inward awareness of right action about any person, or relative to some desired good, is spiritual treatment. (See *treatment—mentally knowing.*)

treatment—transcend the condition See *transcend.*

treatment, turning within in See *turning within.*

treatment—will and willingness See *will and willingness.*

Tree of Life Represents that which, rooted in experience, has its branches in heaven. Represents man as bringing forth the fruits of Spirit through experience. The Tree of Life as the Cross represents the Divine Ray passing through the central beam and expanding outward through the crossbeam into experience.

Tree of the knowledge of good and evil Refers to individuality and self-choice. Also refers to the mind eating from the fruit of a belief in duality.

tribal gods Any particular conception of God held by a group of people which is inconsistent with the nature of Reality.

Trinity See *Holy Trinity; Father, Son.*

true (the)—translating the false into See *translating.*

trusting the Christ Complete confidence in the Principle of the creative Spirit within us.

Truth In its universal sense "The Truth" means God, Spirit, Reality; in a lesser sense the word *truth* designates anything that is true—a psychological truth, a spiritual truth, a physical truth. (See *believing the Truth and believing in Truth; knowing the Truth; no reason; practicing the Truth.*)

Truth, alone with   A spiritual mind practitioner must realize that Truth is not only all Power, it is also the only Performer. Truth operates wherever it is recognized. The practitioner's treatment or mental work takes place in his own consciousness, in his own contemplation of the Truth, immediately available and instantly effective. He works alone in his own consciousness with the Truth of Being.

Truth, demonstrating the   See *demonstrating the Truth.*

Truth dissolves error   The creative activity of thought operating on a higher level of consciousness dissolves the form which a lower operation of the same creative power has projected. (See *impersonalizing error; error, to dissolve.*)

Truth, establishing   See *establishing Truth.*

Truth is both Cause and Effect   Just as an image held in front of a mirror casts a reflection, which reflection is an effect of the image, so Truth or consciousness comes before the image and creates it or projects it. Hence both the image before the mirror and its reflection in the mirror (which constitute cause and effect) are superseded by that which, being neither cause nor influenced by any effect, is, in a certain sense, neither cause nor effect but at the same time all Cause and Effect—cause and effect are projected by It. (See *Spirit is both.*)

Truth is that which heals   It is written that the prayer of faith shall heal the sick and God will raise him up. The prayer of faith means mental compliance with the conditions which make possible the new influx of life. It is the new influx of life which heals. This would be true in reference to any law in nature. We use the laws, the laws execute themselves. (See *prayer of faith.*)

Truth known by what it does   See *we know.*

Truth known is demonstrated A recognition and acceptance of that which is True automatically demonstrates its own answer.

Truth of being Refers to the theory that all being is spiritual; that man is inseparably unified with the Original Creative Principle; that his work is creative because his word is God in him. Knowledge of one's unity with God.

Truth realized is as effective as is the embodiment of our realization It is not just what we say, but what we inwardly understand that gives power to our words.

"truth (the) shall make you free" This refers to the understanding that Truth, known, automatically demonstrates Itself. To understand, believe in, accept, and no longer deny right action is to project right action. Jesus is referring to the spiritual recognition of the unity of the Law of Life, the knowledge of which frees us from the bondage of unbelief.

Truth, Spirit of See *Spirit of Truth.*

Truth, unassailable See *unassailable.*

tuning into Good Tuning the dial of thought to harmony, peace, power, and perfection.

tuning into power Meditating upon the thought of spiritual power until the mind, by acceptance, consciously unifies with Power. From this type of meditation new ideas are born.

turning to God in thought Centering the thought on the idea of peace, happiness, wholeness, completion, and perfection. Turning in thought from the limited to the limitless, from the unholy to the holy.

turning within in mental treatment Turning to the realization that Spirit is at the center of everything, perfect, complete, and whole; turning from the condition to the cause which will create a new condition.

twice-born This term indicates being delivered into the world of Spirit—that is, into unity with the Supreme—while being embodied in physical form. The birth of consciousness from this limited perspective to a realization of the union of all life. A consciousness of the universe as a spiritual system of which man is some part. A consciousness of spirituality, wholeness, and the Kingdom of God here and now.

two ultimate powers impossible If they were identical they would be one and not two; if each were infinite one would cancel the other and nothing would be left.

U

unassailable Truth In such degree as thought functions from the consciousness of an absolute unity of good, there is no possibility of its being interfered with.

unbelief is our acceptance Since unbelief is a mental attitude, even though a negative one, and since the Creative Law must react to our thought exactly as we think it, even unbelief uses the Law of Cause and Effect creatively.

unconscious thought Refers to the subjective processes of thought with which we are not consciously familiar. (See *subconscious does.*)

uncovering error Revealing the false mental position.

understand the truth—God heals when we do Just as electric energy becomes a light when properly understood and used, so there is a spiritual law which, believed in, understood, and used, automatically heals.

understanding   See *faith and; faith based on; spiritual understanding; "With all."*

understanding and belief   The difference between believing and hoping; the actual knowing that a definite law of cause and effect operates upon our word.

understanding God at the level of our own consciousness   We understand love only as we embody it. The only meaning that life can have to us is the meaning that it has in and through us. This is why it is necessary, in giving mental treatments, that we believe our own words, that we understand them, appreciate their meaning, and inwardly feel the presence of what these words suggest.

understanding of the Absolute is our relative   Since consciousness is always automatically reflecting itself into conditions, conditions are always revealing the nature of our states of consciousness.

unfoldment   See *Principle of.*

unifying with God   The mental reaction of the Oneness of all Life.

unity   The Oneness of all life. Man's inseparable union with nature, with the Christ Mind, and with God. (See *multiplicity.*)

Unity, Law of   See *Law of Unity.*

unity necessitates ultimate harmony   Unity means One, Indivisible, Whole, Complete, Perfect, hence adjustment of apparent parts to the whole, and the whole to apparent parts in harmony. (See *harmony.*)

unity—subjective unity between all people   See *subjective unity.*

universal idea   That which must be so. In the final analysis, that which reason compels us to accept.

Universal Intelligence An aspect of Universal Mind, which denotes responsiveness. This is the principle involved in all mental and spiritual healing—the intelligent response of the atoms in the physical structure; also the Intelligence of the Creative Law that knows how to bring harmony into manifestation.

Universal Mind Spirit, God, the Absolute. (See *subjective mind, our: as a.*)

Universal (the) must become the individual in order to be individualized Life can work for us only by working through us in the act of Itself becoming the thing It does.

Universal Presence The Spirit manifesting in and through everything; the Creative Intelligence responding to us from everything; Omnipresence.

Universal Principles All laws of nature are universal, evenly distributed, and ever present.

Universe See *spiritual universe.*

Universe as a dual unity consists of an active and a passive principle This does not imply duality but emphasizes the necessity that there shall be an active principle consciously at work and a receptive Law obeying its consciousness.

Universe as a spiritual and mental system The entire universe consists of pure, absolute Intelligence, Consciousness, and Self-Awareness. This is what constitutes the spiritual universe. Spiritual awareness produces mechanical law which is the Law of Mind in action. This is the mental universe. All creation is a result of the spiritual operating upon or through the mental as Idea. Man is a spiritual, mental being, reproducing this whole cosmic order in his own life.

universe (our) as our meditation See *our universe.*

Universe as the meditation of God The visible universe is an effect of the Divine Creative Imagination.

Universe is not divided against Itself Since the Spirit is One, an undivided and indivisible unity, then the Law of Spirit likewise is a unity. This Unity delivers Its power only on terms of Its own nature, which nature It never contradicts. There cannot be two ultimates, else one would neutralize the other and we should have chaos instead of cosmos.

Universe, true perspective of There is no material universe, if by material we mean a universe opposed to, other than, or different from a spiritual universe.

Un-Nameable One The everlasing Reality from which all things come; the Fountain of all things and the Root of all things.

unwavering mind A mind that does not move from the subject taken for meditation. One-pointed, steady, firm.

V

Vedas Sacred books of India, of ancient Truth and Wisdom.

"Vengeance is mine saith the Lord" Refers to the Law of Cause and Effect.

vibration Oscillating waves in ether. Everything that exists is Original Substance, or ether, in different rates of vibration. The world that seems so solid, so static, is a dynamo of activity, forever changing every second of time. No particle of man's body is the same from one moment to another. Each stands in the center of a moving, vibrating world, and the rate of the vibration depends upon the person. The higher and finer vibrations are the results of harmonious, joyous thought. The heavier and harsher vibrations occur when one is out of tune with the One Indwelling Presence that holds each in His true note of harmony. Man radiates what he will out into the ethers through the vibrational forces of his being. His very thought extends to the outermost reaches of the universe through this Law of Vibration. (See *etheric vibrations*.)

virgins, the wise and foolish Refers to the wise or foolish use of the Power within us. The wise virgins represent those who are conscious that the Presence of Spirit and the Power of Life is within them. The foolish virgins represent those who have exhausted their objective energies and do not realize the spring of life welling up in their own soul, and therefore believe that they must live by external aid.

visible and Invisible Refers to the realm of Mind and Spirit, which is the Invisible Cause, and the realm of form, which is an effect. (See *"Invisible things."*)

vision See *spiritual vision*.

visualization To make a mental picture, which facilitates realization. To picture a thing clearly, specifically, through the power of the imagination, in order to create through thought.

W

"Wages of sin is death" Refers to the necessity that all error shall finally destroy itself.

"Walk in Spirit" Live, move, and have your being in conscious realization of the Divine Presence.

water turned into wine   Symbolizes the transmuting Power of Spiritual Energy.

we cannot contract the Absolute but we can expand the finite   We cannot break any of nature's laws, but we can always use them in a less limited way.

we cannot experience more than we have embodied, but we can increase our embodiment   Today we are a result of what we were yesterday. Today, however, we may increase our understanding, hence tomorrow we shall experience more good.

we heal not persons but thoughts   The Spiritual Man is never sick. Spiritual healing consists of changing psychological thought patterns.

we know what Truth is by what It does   We have no way of judging Causation other than by observing Its effects.

we neither spiritualize matter nor psychologize Spirit   Spiritual mind healing is based upon the theory that there is no material universe and no physical universe separated from Mind; that all things and events are Mind in form, hence there is no material universe to spiritualize and no material condition to become spiritualized. It is also a mistake to suppose that we psychologize or mentally influence through suggestion. Instead of psychologizing we recognize the Presence of a Creative Principle of perfection at the center of everything. This is not suggestion but realization. (See *spiritualizing*.)

"we walk by faith, not by sight"   Interior awareness or spiritual intuition transcends physical vision; to have an inward seeing. It is necessary for any scientific mind, no matter what his science may be, to rely upon the principle of such science; which principle, of course, is always invisible. (See *faith—we*.)

"Wells of salvation"   Man's inner spiritual nature.

what is loosed on earth shall be loosed in heaven Death changes nothing; we continue as we are.

"Whatsoever things ye desire" Implies that it was the belief of Jesus that it is perfectly proper for man to pray for, or demonstrate, anything he desires, provided his desire is constructive and in no way contradicts the unity of good. (See *desire*.)

"Whatsoever ye shall bind on earth shall be bound in heaven" The transition through which we pass in physical death does not necessarily change our mental images.

"Whatsoever ye would that men should do to you, do ye even so to them" Refers to the Law of Cause and Effect.

"When thou prayest enter into thy closet" Turn entirely within to the Invisible Cause which produces all visible manifestation.

"When ye stand praying, forgive" The Divine Forgivingness is delivered to us only as we first forgive—this is cause and effect.

"Where your treasure is there will your heart be" We give our whole attention to that which, in our estimation, is of the greatest value to us.

"Whereon the soles of your feet shall tread shall be yours" We occupy the land which our spiritual vision beholds.

"Who hath seen me hath seen the Father" The true or highest nature of man reveals God.

"Whose seed was in itself, after his kind" The Divine Idea set in motion reproduces Itself after Its kind.

"Whosoever hath, to him shall be given. Whosoever hath not, from him shall be taken away" A consciousness of abundance attracts more abundance, while fear of lack attracts limitation.

"Whosoever shall do the will of my Father . . . the same is my brother" We are all one and united with each other in Spirit.

will and representation A philosophic term meaning Mind and manifestation.

will and willingness Spiritual mind treatment is not an exercise of will power, but rather of a mental willingness to believe that the Law responds to our word.

will as a directive but not a creative power The office of the will is to choose, decide, deliberately exercise volition, etc. It is the Principle of Mind Itself which creates; our part, having directed the Power, is not to compel It but to permit It—not will, but belief and willingness.

Will of God The Nature of God. That is, if the Nature of God is peace, then the Will of God must be like His Nature, hence the Will of God must be peace. (See *"Thy will."*)

"Wilt thou be made whole?" The inevitable invitation of Reality to all that lives. The proclamation of Truth. The self-evident necessity that Life Itself must be whole. Will we accept it?

wisdom—"God is wisdom, therefore man is wise" Man reflects, embodies, or incarnates the Wisdom which God is.

"With all thy getting get understanding" The most important thing of all is the realization of our relationship with the Infinite.

"with the pure thou wilt show thyself pure and with the froward thou wilt show thyself froward" Has reference to the Law of Cause and Effect, which responds to us by corresponding with our mental attitudes.

Witness, the inner All have a spiritual interior awareness ever seeking expression through intuition. This is the drive back of evolution.

"wolf shall dwell with the lamb" The understanding that God is in all things manifesting in such complete unity that there is no longer any hurt in anything.

womb of nature Esoteric term referring to the Creative Principle impregnated by the Divine Ideas.

word See *law and; "So shall."*

word becomes flesh Subjective mental states always tend to take external form, thus spiritual realization passes through law into experience. (See *word made.*)

word does not have to reach any objective place, it merely describes the place Since there is one medium of Mind, we do not send out thoughts; we merely set thought in motion in this Mind by making certain statements about a person or a condition.

word does not speak the Power into existence but into form The word, acting as a mold, makes possible the experience which the word suggests, but it never creates either the Living Presence or the Dynamic Law which flows through the word.

word, I speak my Refers to spiritual mind treatment, where one declares spiritual Truth for himself or another.

word is a mold Ideas automatically reflect themselves into Mind.

"word (the) is very nigh . . . in thy mouth" The creative Power of Life is within and never external to us. It is every word we speak.

word made flesh The Divine Creative Word taking form. This cosmic process is reenacted in man. (See *word becomes.*)

word of authority The word which has unqualified reliance upon good.

Word of God Any self-evident Truth which, by the nature of its being, proclaims itself to be what it is. The nature of God in execution. The Law of the Mind of God in action. The Divine Creative Principle at work. The self-evident necessity somewhat similar to the Divine Ideas of Plato. In treatment, the Word of God means the power of the Creative Spirit operating at the level of our consciousness. (See *worlds were.*)

word of healing Any word implying spiritual perfection and consciously directed for some specific reason.

word, power of the spoken It is not the word, but the consciousness of its meaning, the thought back of it, that gives it power.

word, to speak your Conscious use of the Creative Power of Mind for definite purposes.

words (our) are life if we believe that they are In analytical psychology, words without meaning have no power, and in spiritual mind practice it is useless to use words unless they have a deep meaning in our own consciousness.

words, find your own Spiritual mind practice does not use formulas, although it may use suggested methods of procedure. All such suggested methods, however, must have a definite meaning to the one using them. It is better to use your own words.

words have power commensurate with their conviction It is useless merely to state that God is good, unless, accompanying such statement, there is an inner conviction of truth.

words (your) must convey something to your thought In

mental treatment the words, thoughts, or expressions used by a practitioner have no magic of themselves; their power consists, not in the words, but in the conviction spoken through them.

words of thanksgiving, praise, gratitude, etc. Grateful and joyful recognition releases spiritual and mental energies which negative states of consciousness do not contact.

words, transforming power of See *transforming.*

world as a reflection of God Reflection, of itself, is nothingness; it has neither substance nor intelligence of its own. Thus it is not self-creative but projected, hence always obedient to that which projects it. The Creator is mirrored in creation, but not caught by it or limited to it.

world (our) is our view of Reality Even though Reality is Infinite, that which we image from It, at any particular time, represents what we have accepted of the limitless Principle of our own being.

world, objective See *subjective world as cause of.*

world, subjective See *subjective world.*

world without end Creation is an eternal process.

worlds See *higher and.*

worlds were framed by the word of God The universe is a result of the meditation of the Creative Spirit.

Y

"Ye are Christ's and Christ is God's" *Christ* means the Divine Sonship, and the *Divine Sonship* means God in man. (See *Christ.*)

"Ye ask and receive not because ye ask amiss" By *ask amiss* Jesus refers to asking contrary to the Divine Nature. For example, we cannot ask love to become hate; we cannot ask life to become death; we cannot ask harmony to destroy; who takes up the sword will perish by it; etc.

"Ye cannot serve God and mammon" As it is impossible to walk two ways at once, so it is impossible to believe in both good and evil without becoming confused.

"Yea, yea; nay, nay" Acceptance of the Truth and denial of its opposite.

Yoga The practice of meditation and study to bring the individual life into a conscious unity with the Center of Life —God. Yoga is a conscious union with the Supreme Source of Being. There are several Paths of Yoga, as taught by the eastern philosophies. The Path of Attainment is divided into three Paths: (1) Raja Yoga, the will, mental. (2) Karma Yoga, work and action. (3) Gnani Yoga, wisdom. Also there is Hatha Yoga, the Yoga of physical well-being; and Bhakti Yoga, or the Path of Devotion, the Path of Religion.

you are God The life in, of, and around man is One Life. The indivisible unity of all life. The Divine exists everywhere, therefore at the center of man's being.

your Real Self is not evil The True Self is neither sick nor sinful, nor can it become destroyed. To declare this Truth about the self is scientific mental practice.

"Your sins have hid his face from you" We do not see the face of Reality through confusion, negation, evil, etc.

your true self-hood Christ, the Mind of God, or the Divine Presence within you. Your individualization of the Spirit, which represents a separate, but not separated, unique presentation of the Creative Whole.

172